Eating
in the Light
the

Also by Doreen Virtue

Books/Calendar/Kits/Oracle Board

Living Pain Free (with Robert Reeves, N.D.; available March 2015)

Angels of Love (with Grant Virtue; available February 2015)

The Lightworker's Survival Guide
(with Charles Virtue; available January 2015)

Angel Lady (available November 2014)

The Big Book of Angel Tarot
(with Radleigh Valentine; available July 2014)

Angels of Abundance (with Grant Virtue; available May 2014)

Angel Dreams (with Melissa Virtue; available April 2014)

Angel Astrology 101 (with Yasmin Boland; available March 2014)

Angel Detox (with Robert Reeves, N.D.)

Assertiveness for Earth Angels

How to Heal a Grieving Heart (with James Van Praagh)

The Essential Doreen Virtue Collection

Whispers from Above 2014 Calendar

The Miracles of Archangel Gabriel

Mermaids 101

Flower Therapy (with Robert Reeves, N.D.)

Mary, Queen of Angels

Saved by an Angel

The Angel Therapy® Handbook

Angel Words (with Grant Virtue)

Archangels 101

The Healing Miracles of Archangel Raphael

The Art of Raw Living Food (with Jenny Ross)

Signs from Above (with Charles Virtue)

The Miracles of Archangel Michael

Angel Numbers 101

Solomon's Angels (a novel)

My Guardian Angel (with Amy Oscar)

Angel Blessings Candle Kit
(with Grant Virtue; includes booklet, CD, journal, etc.)

Thank You, Angels! (children's book with Kristina Tracy)

Healing Words from the Angels

How to Hear Your Angels

Realms of the Earth Angels

Fairies 101

Daily Guidance from Your Angels

Divine Magic

How to Give an Angel Card Reading Kit

Angels 101

Angel Guidance Board

Goddesses & Angels

Crystal Therapy (with Judith Lukomski)

Connecting with Your Angels Kit (includes booklet, CD, journal, etc.)

Angel Medicine

The Crystal Children

Archangels & Ascended Masters

Earth Angels

Messages from Your Angels

Angel Visions II

The Care and Feeding of Indigo Children

Healing with the Fairies

Angel Visions

Divine Prescriptions

Healing with the Angels

"I'd Change My Life If I Had More Time"

Divine Guidance

Chakra Clearing

Angel Therapy®

The Lightworker's Way

Constant Craving A–Z

Constant Craving

The Yo-Yo Diet Syndrome

Losing Your Pounds of Pain

Audio/CD Programs

The Healing Miracles of Archangel Raphael

Angel Therapy® Meditations

Archangels 101 (abridged audio book)

Fairies 101 (abridged audio book)

Goddesses & Angels (abridged audio book)

Angel Medicine (available as both 1- and 2-CD sets)

Angels among Us (with Michael Toms)

Messages from Your Angels (abridged audio book)

Past-Life Regression with the Angels

Divine Prescriptions

The Romance Angels

Connecting with Your Angels

Manifesting with the Angels

Karma Releasing

Healing Your Appetite, Healing Your Life

Healing with the Angels

Divine Guidance

Chakra Clearing

DVD Program

How to Give an Angel Card Reading

Oracle Cards (divination cards and guidebook)

Angel Answers Oracle Cards (available October 2015)

Guardian Angel Tarot Cards
(with Radleigh Valentine; available April 2015)

Earth Angels Tarot Cards
(with Radleigh Valentine; available December 2014)

Past Life Oracle Cards
(with Brian Weiss, M.D.; available October 2014)

Cherub Angel Cards for Children (available June 2014)

Angels of Abundance Tarot Cards
(with Radleigh Valentine; available May 2014)

Talking to Heaven Mediumship Cards (with James Van Praagh)

Archangel Power Tarot Cards (with Radleigh Valentine)

Flower Therapy Oracle Cards (with Robert Reeves)

Indigo Angel Oracle Cards (with Charles Virtue)

Angel Dreams Oracle Cards (with Melissa Virtue)

Mary, Queen of Angels Oracle Cards

Angel Tarot Cards (with Radleigh Valentine and Steve A. Roberts)

The Romance Angels Oracle Cards

Life Purpose Oracle Cards

Archangel Raphael Healing Oracle Cards

Archangel Michael Oracle Cards

Angel Therapy® Oracle Cards

Magical Messages from the Fairies Oracle Cards

Ascended Masters Oracle Cards

Daily Guidance from Your Angels Oracle Cards

Saints & Angels Oracle Cards

Magical Unicorns Oracle Cards

Goddess Guidance Oracle Cards

Archangel Oracle Cards

Magical Mermaids and Dolphins Oracle Cards

Messages from Your Angels Oracle Cards

Healing with the Fairies Oracle Cards

Healing with the Angels Oracle Cards

All of the above are available at your local bookstore,
or may be ordered by visiting:

Hay House USA: www.hayhouse.com®
Hay House Australia: www.hayhouse.com.au
Hay House UK: www.hayhouse.co.uk
Hay House South Africa: www.hayhouse.co.za
Hay House India: www.hayhouseco.in

Doreen's website: www.AngelTherapy.com

Eating
in
the Light

Making the Switch to Veganism
on Your Spiritual Path

UPDATED EDITION

DOREEN VIRTUE &
BECKY BLACK, M.F.T., R.D.

HAY HOUSE, INC.
Carlsbad, California • New York City
London • Sydney • Johannesburg
Vancouver • Hong Kong • New Delhi

To the animal kingdom
— Doreen Virtue

To Nick and Irie
— Becky Black

CONTENTS

Chapter 1: Why Go Vegan?. 1

Chapter 2: Food, Energy, and Life Force 35

Chapter 3: Making the Transition 59

Chapter 4: Vegan Myths Debunked 75

Chapter 5: Eating Wholesomely 93

Appendix A: Optimal Intake Range for
Vitamins and Minerals 129

Appendix B: Care of the Earth 133

Resources 139

Bibliography. 145

About the Authors. 147

CHAPTER ONE

Why Go Vegan?

*"If one is trying to practice meditation
and is still eating meat, he would be like
a man closing his ears and shouting loudly,
and then asserting that he heard nothing."*

— FROM THE SURANGAMA SUTRA, A BUDDHIST TEXT

Many spiritually minded people say, "I feel guided to be a vegan." When we ask them for clarification, they say, "Something inside of me is telling me to eat a lighter, plant-based diet. I find that I can't stomach the foods that I used to enjoy. It's like I can no longer tolerate meat or processed foods." So, many of us are becoming vegans, and studies show that the consumption of meat—red meat, specifically—is falling every year.

What is the link between being on the spiritual path and a changing relationship with food? It has little to do with a desire to lose weight, although most people on vegan diets inevitably shed pounds and inches. Most spiritually minded people seem to choose vegan or near-vegan diets because some inner guidance directs them to do so.

In this book, we'll explore the connection between spirituality and veganism. We'll also look at some very earthly, grounded methods that will help you adopt a vegan lifestyle. To be . . . or not to be . . . a vegan is a soulful decision.

The Spiritual History of Veganism

Veganism has an ancient history, much of it tied into spirituality, philosophy, and religion. Eastern religions such as Hinduism and Buddhism embrace vegetarianism as a path to attaining bliss, achieving optimum health, making a greater connection with the Creator, and honoring the sacredness of animals' lives to a greater extent. The Buddhists and Hindus also believe that karmic law makes any suffering that we cause—to animals or humans—come back to haunt us at a future time.

Other Eastern religions that espouse vegetarianism include the Sikhs, who focus on living ethically and nonviolently; the Krishna devotees, who believe that vegetarianism is a way to reduce violent acts in the world; and the Jains, who are strict vegans because they believe animals used for dairy products or meat are made to suffer needlessly. The Baha'i faith doesn't require its members to become vegetarians; however, its spiritual texts prophesize, "The food of the future will be fruit and grains. The time will come when meat will no longer be eaten. Our natural food is that which comes out of the ground. The people will gradually develop up to the condition of this natural food."

The Essenes, an ancient mystical Jewish group who wrote the Dead Sea Scrolls, held vegetarianism as their spiritual law. They especially favored eating raw and uncooked vegetables and legumes. They believed that this way of eating led to optimal health and spiritual cleanliness.

The Greek philosophers Pythagoras and Seneca also promoted veganism as a way to higher consciousness and to avoid adding suffering to the world through animal slaughter. Trappist monks, a sector of the Roman Catholic Church, practice vegetarianism, as do many Orthodox monks and nuns. The Western

Catholic monastic orders are vegetarians because they follow ancient spiritual rules, including the 39th Rule of St. Benedict, which says, "But let all, except the very weak and the sick, abstain altogether from eating the flesh of four-footed animals." Quakers practice vegetarianism out of compassion for animals, and also to help alleviate world hunger, since they quote statistics stating how the world's resources are greatly overused by animals raised for slaughter.

Seventh-Day Adventists practice vegetarianism, and only serve vegetarian foods in their hospitals and restaurant cafés. Their official church stance on vegetarianism is, according to the *Seventh-day Adventist Position Statement on Vegetarian Diets,* "For more than 130 years Seventh-day Adventists (SDAs) have practiced a vegetarian dietary lifestyle because of their belief in the holistic nature of humankind. Whatever is done in eating or drinking should honor and glorify God and preserve the health of the body, mind and spirit."

Some Jewish vegetarian groups interpret the words of Genesis and the Torah to be promoters of vegetarianism. For instance, they quote Genesis 1:29, which says, "Behold, I give you every herb-bearing seed and the fruit of every seed-bearing tree; for you it shall be for food." These groups also say that Jewish law only allows meat-eating if it meets man's "basic needs." Since vegetarian foods meet these needs adequately, meat-eating isn't necessary.

Philosophers and spiritual leaders have also practiced and promoted vegetarianism because they view animal slaughter as inhumane and unnecessary. For instance, Mahatma Gandhi said, "To my mind, the life of a lamb is no less precious than that of a human being. I should be unwilling to take the life of a lamb for the sake of the human body."

Henry David Thoreau, the great American philosopher and author, wrote, "I have no doubt that it is a part of the destiny of the human race, in its gradual improvement, to leave off eating animals." And Albert Einstein, the brilliant physicist, said, "Nothing will benefit human health and increase chances for survival of life on Earth as much as the evolution to a vegetarian diet."

A Deeply Personal Choice

Sometimes, the food journey will take you all the way to becoming a vegan, which means avoiding *all* animal products, including dairy. I (Doreen) have been a complete vegan since 1996. For others, excluding red meat will be the extent of your vegetarianism.

It's important for you to go inward and decide on the level of vegetarianism that's best for you.

It doesn't mean that you must become vegetarian to be "spiritually minded," or that if you eat meat, you are "unspiritual." Being vegetarian doesn't make you *better* than someone who eats meat. It is simply a deeply personal decision, based on many factors that we'll explore in this book.

Most people on the spiritual path find that their appetites change so that they are only craving healthful and humanely created foods. As your spiritual vibrations increase, it becomes more difficult to digest highly processed foods, chemical-laden foods and beverages, and products derived from animals (especially those who were cruelly treated).

It's not always easy being a vegan in a society that is still largely meat based. But if you've felt guided to eliminate or reduce the amount of animal products in your diet, you'll find support and answers in these pages.

The Types of Vegetarians

Occasionally we'll hear someone say, "Oh, a vegetarian is someone who doesn't eat beef"; that is, some people think that vegetarians are people who don't eat meat, and that "meat" consists of beef only. In actuality, beef, pork, turkey, chicken, and fish all fall under the category of *meat.*

There are many types of vegetarians. As you read the list below, meditate upon each type of vegetarian to see which one feels right to you. Or, you may want to approach vegetarianism gradually, and begin with one type of eating and then slowly make your way to veganism. Becoming a vegetarian involves more than changing your eating patterns. It's a lifestyle choice.

Vegetarian Type	Foods Consumed	Foods Avoided
Lacto	Grains, legumes, vegetables, nuts, seeds, dairy	Beef, pork, poultry, fish, eggs
Ovo	Grains, legumes, vegetables, nuts, seeds, eggs	Beef, pork, poultry, fish, dairy
Lacto-ovo	Grains, legumes, vegetables, nuts, seeds, dairy, eggs	Beef, pork, poultry, fish
Pollo	Grains, legumes, vegetables, nuts, seeds, poultry	Beef, pork, fish, dairy, eggs
Pesco	Grains, legumes, vegetables, nuts, seeds, fish	Beef, pork, poultry, dairy, eggs

Lacto-ovo-pollo-pesco	Grains, legumes, vegetables, nuts, seeds, dairy, eggs, chicken, fish	Beef, pork
Vegan	Grains, legumes, vegetables, nuts, seeds	Beef, pork, poultry, fish, dairy, eggs, animal by-products (casein, whey, honey)
Fruitarian	Fruits and fruit juices	Everything but fruit
Raw food–ists	Uncooked vegetables, fruits, and nuts	Beef, pork, poultry, eggs, fish, dairy, cooked vegetables, cooked fruits, and cooked nuts

Veganism and the Law of Attraction

There is a spiritual law threaded throughout our universe that applies to all of us: "Our thoughts create our reality." If we think thoughts of love and success, we attract, notice, and create loving and successful situations. If, on the other hand, we focus upon negativity, we experience the world as negative.

Taking up a spiritual practice invariably makes us more positive-minded. We start to see the good in other people, and the blessing within each challenge. We begin to feel safe, because our spiritual practices help us realize that we're one with God, and surrounded by angels who love us.

This more positive approach to living can create huge changes in our lives! We treat ourselves better, avoid negative people and situations, and generally raise our standards. For some individuals, this might mean leaving a job and embarking on a self-employment venture, or it might mean spending less time with negative friends or relatives.

Many people on the spiritual path begin to crave healthier situations. Perhaps you've noticed these changes in yourself. For example, you may no longer enjoy or tolerate violent movies. Or, you may feel inclined to spend more time in nature. These changes occur because of the Law of Attraction. Here's a story that illustrates this point.

LeAnn and Debra

LeeAnn had been friends with Debra since they were teenagers. After LeeAnn's divorce, she began attending a study group that focused on spiritual and metaphysical books. Each week following her study group, LeeAnn felt happier and more peaceful, and she made friends with other members of the group.

LeeAnn started to notice that whenever she was with Debra, she felt down and depressed. She remarked to another friend, "I never realized how negative Debra is. I feel guilty, but I've been avoiding her lately."

Lee Ann was experiencing the Law of Attraction. It's not that Debra was "bad," or that Lee-Ann was "better" than her friend. It's just that her new spiritual activities opened up her higher chakra energy centers. This naturally made her attracted to people and situations who were operating out of this higher area.

LeeAnn decided to heal this situation by inviting Debra to attend her spiritual study group. By doing so, her friend could benefit from the group members' positive energy as well as the material in the books that they were studying.

The Stages of Veganism

Another internal shift experienced by those of us on the spiritual path relates to the way we crave and digest foods. Generally, we go through a series of stages on our way to becoming a vegetarian or vegan. For example, a woman named Andrea had been meditating and taking yoga classes for six months when she stated, "I find that I can no longer digest highly processed foods. I used to love doughnuts and pastries, but now they just give me a stomachache."

For those of you who are new to the spiritual path, like Andrea, your first change in eating patterns might be an inability to tolerate sugar or white flour. Your body begins to reflect the higher vibrational frequency of a spiritually minded soul. It may continue to crave "junk food," but your stomach can no longer digest it easily.

The next step could be an actual change in your food cravings. For example, we know of a woman named Brenda who had been studying *A Course in Miracles* for a year and a half when she noticed significant changes in this regard. "I used to crave sugary chocolate every month, right before starting my period," Brenda said, "but it's incredible that I'm just not craving chocolate candy at all anymore."

The cravings for junk food may recur during stressful times, but for the most part, those on the spiritual path experience an overall reduction in junk-food cravings. When indulging in junk food, people often notice strong negative reactions, such as stomach-aches, fatigue, headaches, or edginess.

The next stages of dietary changes continue to be directed from within. "I feel guided to avoid or reduce these foods," is the most common way in which these changes are described. At this stage, many people give up, avoid, or reduce their consumption of red meat. Just as with other life changes inspired by being on the spiritual path, eliminating red meat from the diet happens through the Law of Attraction.

That may be enough of a change for some who are on the spiritual path. For others, though, their body next rejects eating fowl. They end up reducing the amount of chicken and turkey they eat, or they may eliminate it altogether. Or, they may only eat "free-range" birds, who were humanely treated during their lives and who weren't given antibiotics, growth hormones, and genetically modified food (which are all passed on to whoever eats the bird or its eggs).

At this point, some will stay in this semi-vegetarian state. Others will totally avoid meat—or all animal products. They will give up fish next, then go on to eliminate dairy products. The choice is a personal one, based upon many possible considerations, including some of the following.

Environmental Concerns

If you're on the spiritual path, you have most likely developed some conscious connections with Mother Earth. Developing an awareness of the environment is a natural extension of listening to your inner voice. You become more conscientious about littering, polluting, and toxins in the environment.

This inevitably leads to changes in your behavior—for instance, going to the trouble of picking up someone else's litter, or buying your cleaning supplies at health-food stores. Food safety (including safety of the animals' food supply) and the impact made by the raising of livestock are still other reasons why people, in increasing numbers, are "going veggie." Have the animals been fed foods that contain pesticides, antibiotics, genetically modified organisms (GMOs), or disease-causing bacteria? How many hormones have the animals been given?

"Environmentally, the livestock population of the United States today consumes enough grain and soybeans to feed over five times the entire human population of the country," the Institute for Food and Development reports. "We feed these animals over 80 percent of the corn we grow, and over 95 percent of the oats."

Lester Brown, of the Overseas Development Council, has estimated that if Americans were to reduce their meat consumption by only 10 percent, it would free more than 12 million tons of grain annually for human needs. He reminds us that every day, 40,000 children starve to death in the world. Of course, we wouldn't necessarily feed these children the unused grain; however, if we reduced our meat and poultry consumption, we would increase grain and land available that could be used to grow food for hungry and starving people.

Then there's water use. To produce a single pound of meat takes an average of 2,500 gallons of water. That's how much water the average family uses in a month. There are many indicators that our planet may experience a water shortage in the near future. You make a major contribution toward averting such a crisis by eliminating or reducing beef consumption in your life.

Treatment of Animals

Two factors create feelings of denial in people when it comes to how we raise and slaughter the animals we eat. One has to do with an animal's intelligence, and the other relates to geography.

First, people tend to think that animals are dumb, and that they will not feel the pain of being slaughtered. Also, by dissociating from the reality of where meat comes from, the bloody details of the slaughter can be ignored, as if they are not part of someone's everyday reality. When one does take these factors into account, though, it becomes increasingly unpleasant to look at a package of cellophane-wrapped meat and realize what kind of life the cow, pig, chicken, lamb, or turkey must have endured.

Most animals raised for meat, dairy products, eggs, leather, or fur suffer brutal lives and deaths. These creatures are known as "factory-farmed animals." They aren't raised on quaint country farms with white picket fences. Instead, they are crammed into tiny, uncomfortable pens. Often, they are unable to turn around, or even scratch themselves in these little quarters. Big-business farming turns huge profits by producing as many animals, using as little space, as possible. On chicken farms, the crowded conditions breed violence, as chickens continually peck at each other. As a result, their beaks are chopped off (without the use of anesthesia) to prevent them from injuring each other.

On commercial egg farms, millions of boy chicks are put on conveyer belts, where they fall over the side into crushing machines. That's because males won't produce eggs, so their lives are deemed worthless and their pain is irrelevant.

Baby cows, also known as "veal," are kept in a tightly confined space, chained to a bin for their brief lives. The less they move, the more tender the veal, thus the more money their flesh commands. Can you imagine three months of being bedridden, and only being allowed to move from side to side? This is most likely how a baby cow feels.

Lobsters may not be as cute and cuddly as baby cows, but they definitely feel pain from inhumane treatment and slaughter. With rubber bands around their claws, lobsters are kept in crammed supermarket tanks. To reduce employee labor needed to clean the tanks, lobsters are not fed in their "death row" prison cells while waiting to be boiled alive.

Livestock are raised in incredibly cruel conditions. Their slaughter is even more inhumane due to their sensitivity and intelligence. For example, when pigs are about to be slaughtered, they know that death is pending. Pigs have sensitive noses that smell the blood of the pigs that have gone before and register all of their squeals of pain.

As a matter of fact, experts say that pigs are more intelligent than dogs, and anyone who has owned a dog knows that they sense danger. Therefore, pigs, as well as cows, baby cows (aka veal), chickens, turkeys, and lamb, probably register the danger that floats in the air prior to their demise. To deal with the bristly nature of a pig's skin, most slaughterhouses boil the pigs alive. Chickens are normally boiled alive, too, as part of the de-feathering process.

When cows are slaughtered, their four legs are shackled, and then they're shot in the head. Before they can drop to the ground, they are hoisted into the air, after which their bellies are sliced open. Some may say, "No big deal; they've been shot." But sometimes the slaughterhouse worker's aim is off. You can imagine the rest. The stress of these killing procedures causes animals to release brain chemicals into their bloodstream. One of these chemicals, adrenaline, is popularly known as the "fight-or-flight" hormone. Adrenaline surges through the blood and into the muscles so the animal can run. It's like the rush you get when you're watching a scary movie. All of a sudden, your heart starts to race, and your palms sweat. This, too, happens with the animals. All that adrenaline gets lodged into their muscles, and in turn, we eat this muscle, which is otherwise known as "meat."

When we eat inhumanely treated animals, we are literally *eating the energy of pain*. We are ultimately composed of energy, and everything about our body can be broken down into energy. When we eat meat that is saturated with fear, we absorb the energy and chemicals of fear, which in turn, is held in the body. Praying, blessing the food, and offering gratitude for our food is vital in decreasing the impact that this fear energy has upon our body.

Another option is to purchase "free-range" animals and dairy products. Available in better health-food stores or from your local farmer, these are high-quality meats, cheeses, eggs, and such from humanely treated animals. Free-range animals are purportedly raised in stress-free environments, with plenty of room for movement. They aren't given growth hormones, the way that factory-farmed animals normally are.

Free-range animals and their by-products generally cost more than their factory-farmed equivalents, but you're investing in the humane treatment of animals, and also in your health. That brings up another benefit of becoming a vegan: You'll save money on your grocery bill when you reduce or eliminate meat or dairy from your diet.

What about Leather, Fur, Silk, and Feathers?

Being a vegan isn't just a diet. It's a lifestyle. It means being consciously aware of how your purchases affect animals and other people. Vegans are highly sensitive to energy, and need to avoid anything that reeks of competition, violence, or other harshness. For that reason, most vegans don't wear or use leather or other animal products.

After all, it's not like the old days when indigenous peoples would commune with wild animals for food and skins. These days, leather, fur, feathers, and silk involve heinous cruelty. Since red-meat consumption is down among Americans, many cattle ranchers are turning to leather production to maintain their income. Those who are leaning toward veganism because of environmental and animal-rights concerns need to remember that buying and wearing leather products contributes both to environmental stress and animal suffering.

Recent investigations and news reports have revealed that in China, pet dogs and cats are being stolen as a free source of leather. The animals are skinned alive for their pelts. Many of the inexpensive China-made leather and fur products are actually made from cats and dogs these days. Awareness and reading labels helps you avoid financing this cruelty!

Many people rationalize that it's okay to use animal skins, fur, and feathers because the animals were killed for food anyway. This may or may not be true. As just discussed, cats and dogs are increasingly killed for their pelts. And many cows are slaughtered primarily for their skin (leather), as well as animals killed for their fur (such as rabbits, chinchilla, and mink). Estimates are that 50 to 80 percent of goose-down products (comforters, coats, pillows, and so forth) come from "live pluck" situations where feathers are ripped out of living geese, despite the pain, injury, and death that this causes. Wool is also often cruelly shorn from sheep, leaving them with wounds. Many vegans avoid the use of silk, which is usually created at the cruel expense of silk worms. The exception is "cruelty-free silk," which you can find with an Internet search of this phrase. Wool, cashmere, pashmina, and angora are also frequently stripped from living animals or those killed in cruel ways.

Ethical and Eco-Friendly Alternatives

Fortunately, there are ethical companies that supply beautiful vegan alternatives to leather, fur, and feathers. These products are much more sophisticated and fashionable than in the old days. A simple search of "vegan boots," for example, will help you find products that didn't involve animal cruelty.

Be sure to look for eco-friendly vegan products, such as those made by the European companies Novacas, Stella McCartney, or OlsenHaus. In addition, be sure that your products are "fair trade," so that workers were treated and paid fairly. After all, we don't want to finance cruelty to animals *or* to humans—and all too often, the garment industry involves sweatshops and child labor. Do your homework and you'll love the high-vibrating energy of everything you wear, eat, and have in your home.

Living Cruelty-Free

Those who are on the spiritual path are sensitive to others' feelings, and are consciously aware of using gentle words and actions. When you're a vegan, your lifestyle calls you to be aware of how people and animals are treated in the manufacturing of the products you use. The phrase "cruelty-free lifestyle" is used interchangeably with veganism.

Fortunately, those who manufacture ethically are very up front about advertising their cruelty-free practices. The terms to watch for prior to purchasing an item are:

- *Fair trade:* All the workers are treated with compassion and are given fair wages.

- *No animal testing:* Animals weren't strapped down in a laboratory and forced to have the product put into their eyes or other parts of their body.

- *Cruelty-free:* No animal testing *plus* the product is vegan and free of animal by-products.

- *Suitable for vegans (or vegetarians):* This is a phrase to look for when purchasing vitamin supplements. Some vitamins are made from animal products, and some are contained in gelatin (created from cow bones) capsules. Look for vitamins from plant sources in vegetable-based capsules.

In addition, the little symbol of a rabbit silhouette certifies that the product wasn't tested on animals. In the Resources section of this book, you can find the website address for products that have qualified for the Leaping Bunny symbol.

Is "Cage-Free Eggs" Just a Cagey Marketing Term?

If you eat eggs and you're a conscientious consumer who wants to reduce suffering in the world, then it's important to know the definition of terms such as *cage-free* before you spend your money:

Certified humane: The chickens are uncaged indoors, and allowed to engage in their natural behaviors. Forced starvation for molting isn't permitted, but beak-cutting is permitted.

Certified organic: The chickens are uncaged in a warehouse or barn, and have access to the outdoors. The Humane Society says that chickens raised under this term often don't go outside, and cruel practices such as beak-cutting and forced starvation to get the chicken to molt are often used.

Free-farmed: The American Humane Society created this phrase to signify truly compassionate treatment of chickens.

Pasture-fed: Chickens who eat outdoors in pastures. This term is usually reserved for small family-run farms.

Free-range or free-roaming: Chickens have access to the outdoors. However, this term still isn't regulated and one study found that only 15 percent of free-range chickens actually spent time outdoors. Cruel beak-cutting and forced starvation to molt are allowed.

Cage-free: This is a completely unregulated phrase that *might* mean that the chickens have room to spread their wings at some factory farms, while at other industrial farms, the chicken cages have a small opening that they can never get through. Most cage-free chickens spend their lives indoors. Beak-cutting and forced starvation for molting is allowed.

Vegetarian-fed: The chicken's food is more natural, but this term doesn't signify compassionate farm practices.

Regarding unlabeled products, never buy eggs that don't have at least a cage-free status. To do so is to support extremely cruel practices.

None of the above labels are perfect, but of all of them, "free-farmed" has the best overall conditions for chickens. If you can buy your eggs from a local farmers' market, where you can verify that the chickens truly have access to the outdoors, then you're supporting the best possible conditions.

Compassionate eggs may cost a little more than unlabeled eggs, but you'll have the satisfaction of knowing that your family is supporting kindness—and the energy of an egg (or any animal product) that came from kindness is much healthier for everyone who consumes it.

The Humane Society says:

Virtually all hens in commercial egg operations—whether cage or cage-free—come from hatcheries that kill all male chicks shortly after hatching. The males are of no use to the egg industry because they don't lay eggs and aren't bred to grow as large or as rapidly as chickens used in the meat industry. Common methods of killing male chicks include suffocation, gassing and grinding. Hundreds of millions of male chicks are killed at hatcheries each year in the United States.

But Don't Plants Have Feelings, Too?

Some will argue with you that veganism is hypocritical, because plants suffer just as much as animals when consumed. Studies do indicate that plants have feelings. Those of us who are sensitive can actually feel or hear trees screaming in pain when their branches are cut. I (Doreen) grew a basil plant so that I could enjoy the flavor of this herb in my meals. But as the plant grew, I became emotionally attached to it as if it were a pet. I couldn't bear to pull leaves from it, and just kept it as a beautiful houseplant.

Fruitarians only consume fruits and nuts because they contend that these are natural gifts from plants, which do not cause the plant any pain. You can look upon corn, grains, beans, legumes, and other plants in the same way.

Mindfulness of the Body

After compassion, health is certainly one of the major reasons why people become vegan. The direct health benefits of a vegan diet are impressive. Vegans have lower rates of:

- Cancer
- Heart disease
- Diabetes
- Cataracts
- Obesity

🖉 Osteoporosis

🖉 Hypertension

🖉 Gallstones

🖉 Kidney disease and kidney stones

In addition . . .

— **Vegans eat less total fat and less saturated fat than meat-eaters.** High-fat and high-saturated-fat diets are linked to an increased risk of diabetes, heart disease, obesity, and possibly cancer. American omnivores (those who eat both animal and vegetable substances) eat a diet that is 34 to 38 percent fat; lacto-ovo vegetarians (those who eat dairy, but no meat) eat a 30 to 36 percent fat diet; and vegans eat a diet that is about 30 percent fat.

— **Vegans also eat less cholesterol.** Dietary cholesterol raises risk for heart disease and possibly for cancer. American omnivores consume about 400 mg of cholesterol per day, lacto-ovo vegetarians consume about 150 to 300 mg of cholesterol, and vegans exclude foods containing cholesterol.

— **Vegans eat more fiber.** Dietary fiber lowers the risk for cancer and heart disease, helps control blood-glucose levels, and possibly reduces the risk of diabetes. Typical Americans eat only about 12 grams of fiber each day. Vegans eat about 50 to 100 percent more fiber than non-vegans.

— **Vegans consume more antioxidants.** Antioxidants may reduce the risk of cancer, heart disease, and possibly arthritis and cataracts. Dietary antioxidants include vitamin E, vitamin C, and carotenoids, as well as the many phytochemicals in plants. Vegan diets are typically between 50 and 100 percent higher in vitamins C and E than carnivorous diets. In addition, vegan meals are rich in phytochemicals. Phytochemicals have beneficial purposes, such as supporting the immune system; detoxifying/blocking carcinogens from attaching to the body's cells; and acting as antioxidants, which cleanse the bloodstream.

— **Vegans consume adequate protein but less total protein and less animal protein.** Omnivores consume a diet that is 14 to 18 percent protein, lacto-ovo vegetarians consume diets comprising 12 to 14 percent protein, and vegan diets are only 10 to 12 percent protein. Excess protein, especially animal protein, may be linked to a higher risk for osteoporosis, kidney stone formation, and kidney disease. Animal protein may raise blood cholesterol levels.

Studies on Veganism, Vegetarianism, and Health

The China Study is one of the most famous books focusing upon the role that veganism plays in health. The researchers were from Cornell University, Oxford University, and the Chinese Academy of Preventive Medicine. After 40 years of research, lead author T. Colin Campbell concludes: "People who ate the most animal-based foods got the most chronic disease. . . . People who ate the most plant-based foods were the healthiest and tended to avoid chronic disease. These results could not be ignored." The book gives charts and outlines of how chronic disease was healed when animal products were removed from the diet.

A registered dietician named Jack Norris of Vegan Health.com took the time in 2013 to analyze and summarize the major studies on veganism, vegetarianism, and health. Here are some of the salient conclusions he drew:

Compared to meat eaters:

- ⌀ Occasional meat eaters (people who ate meat less than once per week) had a 20 percent reduced rate of dying of heart disease and a 10 percent reduced rate of overall mortality.

🖉 Those who ate no meat other than fish had a 34 percent reduced rate of dying from heart disease and an 18 percent reduced rate of overall mortality.

🖉 Lacto-ovo vegetarians had a 38 percent reduced rate of dying from lung cancer, a 34 percent reduced rate of dying from heart disease, and a 15 percent reduced rate of mortality.

🖉 Vegetarians had a statistically significant, 30 percent reduced risk of heart disease. This finding held even after adjusting for body mass index (BMI) and removing the first two years of follow-up. The researchers believed the difference in heart-disease rates to be due mainly to the lower non-HDL cholesterol levels and systolic blood pressure rates of the vegetarians.

🖉 Vegetarians had a 31 percent lower risk of diverticular disease compared with meat eaters.

🖉 Vegetarians had a 12 percent and vegans had a 15 percent lower rate of death.

🖉 Compared to the non-vegetarians, vegetarians had about half the high blood pressure and diabetes and two-thirds the rheumatoid arthritis

Some of the studies indicated that vegans who use vitamin B_{12} supplements enjoy even better health and longevity, compared to vegans who don't supplement.

Listening to Your Feelings

On the spiritual path, you become more aware of your feelings and thoughts; and meditation, prayer, yoga, and other spiritual practices can help you listen. A natural extension of this effect is to listen to your body's reactions to specific foods and beverages. So, a good starting point for you if you're interested in adopting a healthier diet is to tune in to your body's feedback. For example, eat one food at a time, and chew slowly. Close your eyes, breathe deeply, and notice how your body and emotions feel immediately before eating each particular food.

Do you feel excited, bored, tired, stimulated, or some other emotion as your fork makes its way into your mouth? How do you feel as you chew or swallow the food? Then, notice how you feel *after* you've swallowed. Do you feel any different after the food has been eaten, compared to how you felt before?

A major link between eating and one's spiritual path is to eat foods that nurture and support you. Take the time to experiment with different foods so you can determine which ones truly work for you. Sometimes, the foods we like the best give us the most problems. We could have an intolerance or an allergy to these foods, which triggers eating binges.

If you feel sleepy after a meal, most likely something in your food is not in agreement with you. Many foods give people a roller-coaster ride of sorts. There's the caffeine jolt from the morning coffee; then there's a glass of juice, providing a sugar high; combined with a bowl of cereal with milk, when you may be lactose-intolerant. All of this adds up to a three-hit combination. It's no wonder that many people ride the highs and lows of their food intake all day long.

Other symptoms of food allergies or sensitivities include itchy skin, inflammation and swelling, headaches, and nausea. Your local naturopath or dermatologist can help you accurately identify which ingredients your body is rejecting. Once you adapt an allergen-free diet, you'll enjoy more health and comfort. Many people lose weight after they stop consuming foods to which they are allergic.

With a little practice, you can tune in to how a food will affect you long before you eat it. When you go to the grocery store, run your hands along the boxes and cans of foods. Close your eyes, and notice whether your hands feel cold or warm when you pass them over the different items—including the fresh produce. Ask yourself, *Would this food nurture me if I ate it?* If your hands feel cold in response to this question, the answer is no. Warm hands indicate a yes answer.

You can also ask the food directly if it is healthful or unhealthful for you. Hold the food in your hand, close your eyes, and mentally ask the food (before eating it), *Do you love me?* Your gut feelings or inner voice will immediately give you a yes or no answer, unless you don't want to hear the answer. It's possible to block out inner feedback if you're afraid to hear it.

For instance, let's say that you want to eat a high-fat cheeseburger. You tune in and ask, *Will this food serve me?* Then you say, "I can't hear the answer!" You may not want to hear a no answer because you've decided to eat the cheeseburger regardless of what you hear. Again, it's a personal choice. However, it's important to be honest with yourself and to sit quietly so you can hear or feel the voice of God, Holy Spirit, Jesus, your angels, and your Higher Self. It's equally important to follow the guidance of that inner "voice" or "inner knowing," which will most assuredly lead you toward a healthier, happier, more Spirit-filled life.

CHAPTER TWO

Food, Energy, and Life Force

"To become vegetarian is to step
into the stream which leads to Nirvana."

— BUDDHA

Take a long, deep breath. Right now, that breath of air you just filled your lungs with is being separated into molecules. Each molecule is going in its own direction, in perfect harmony, with Divine perfection. But what causes our lungs to expand and contract, the cells on our skin to reproduce, and our stomach to digest our food? Of course there are physiological

35

reasons that explain all of those processes, but what *supports* the physiology?

There is, without a doubt, a beautiful, benevolent life force that's behind all this. Whatever name you choose to use—God, the Universe, Spirit, the Creator, Allah, Rama—they are just attempts at naming the One—which we are all a part of. Throughout this book, we're using the name *God*, but please feel free to substitute whichever word or term you're comfortable with.

This life force can be felt as energy that we plug into for physical, emotional, and spiritual renewal. Modern-day physicists have shown that, ultimately, we are made up of energy. Our body is not really solid; the molecules are just moving very slowly. We are a part of this life force, along with everything else on this earth. And that includes what we eat.

A scene in the movie *Crocodile Dundee* depicted an aboriginal man who wouldn't eat a steak offered to him because "it has been dead too long." The aborigine knew that the meat had no more life force in it and wasn't worthy of being in his body.

Life Force in Foods

When an apple is growing on a tree, drinking in the sunlight, it is filled with the energy of life. That energy is what we call "life force." Once the apple is picked, it still contains much of its life force. The life force keeps the apple firm, juicy, and sweet. However, several variables can affect its life force:

— **Time.** The longer the apple is off the tree, the less life force it has. Freshly picked produce has the most life force of any food. As the produce's life force wears off over time, it becomes wilted and loses its flavor.

— **Temperature.** The body of an apple in many ways is no different from your body. If you were boiled, microwaved, frozen, or steamed, your body could not survive. In the same way, fruits and vegetables lose their life force as they are cooked or frozen.

— **Preparation.** Similarly, when an apple is juiced or sliced, its life force doesn't last for long. Think of how long an apple slice usually lasts before wilting. Compare this to the length of time that a whole apple lasts without wilting. Anytime we process food, we reduce its life force. When produce is juiced, its life force only stays in the juice for about 20 minutes.

— **Packaging.** Highly processed foods usually come in cans, boxes, or in the freezer. In the same way that your body couldn't survive these unnatural conditions, neither can the life force in foods survive. Whenever you eat a canned or freeze-dried product, it means that the food has no life force.

— **Pain.** Food that comes from animals, including dairy products, carries the energy of how the animal was treated during its life and slaughter. It's not like the old days when Native Americans would connect with the soul of a free-roaming animal before killing and consuming it in its entirety! Today, most animals live extremely pain-filled lives in cramped and cruel conditions. Animal products have very little, if any, life force in them. Eating flesh or dairy products from a pain-filled animal can have a negative effect on you, reducing your ability to utilize life-force energy in general.

— **Pesticides.** *Insecticides* and *herbicides* carry the energy of death, as the words literally contain the suffix that means "kill." Just like ingesting pain energy, when we eat foods that have a pesticide or herbicide residue, the death energy lowers our spiritual frequency and vitality. This includes genetically engineered food (GE), which has insect-killing properties built into the seed and food. For this reason, organic food has more life force than foods grown with genetic modification, herbicides, or pesticides.

— **Size.** Medium-size fresh fruits and vegetables have more life force than those that are small or large. Small produce is too "yin," meaning that its life force is still developing. Large produce is too "yang," meaning that its life force is beyond its peak.

— **Irradiation.** Bacteria are radiated in a process called "irradiation," which also breaks down the life force and DNA of the food.

— **The yin and yang.** Foods that are grown above the ground, in the bright sunshine, have an expanding yang force, while foods grown below the ground, in the Earth Mother, embrace a contracting yin force. Above-ground "yang" foods open our psychic gifts and spiritual energy. The below-ground "yin" foods help to ground us, and are beneficial if you ever feel "spaced-out."

— **Additives.** Preservatives, refined sugar, caffeine, white flour, hormones, and other additives have very little life force. They also have the ability to block us from enjoying our own natural life force.

The result is that we feel sluggish, because we're cut off from our life force. Unfortunately, when we feel tired, we often become careless with our eating habits and eat more fast food and sugary snacks.

When you eat mostly high-life-force foods, you feel more energetic and vital. This additional energy may motivate you to start or escalate an exercise program, which will increase your energy level even more.

Doreen's Experience

"I noticed that when I began feeding my children high-life-force food, especially organic food, their energy shifted. My two sons became sweeter and more loving, and developed an awareness of their emotional and physical well-being. Now that they're adults living on their own, they continue to eat healthfully. I never pushed veganism on them. Instead, I fed them high-life-force foods. My sons made their own decision to continue eating foods that made them feel good."

Prayer and Life-Force Energy

Life-force energy is a form of God, contained within physical forms such as fruits, vegetables, and flesh.

We can prolong and impact the life-force energy within our meals through the use of blessings, prayers, or saying grace.

For instance, if you're a vegetarian and your family still eats meat, you can silently say to the soul of the animal you're cooking, "Thank you for giving your life so that my family may be nourished by your flesh." In this way, you transmute the energy of pain within the meat. This is similar to the ritual that Native Americans once used when hunting. They would silently ask the animal's permission to kill, and would bless the animal for surrendering itself for the sake of feeding the tribe. This is called "Give Away."

It's also a good idea to bless the animals who provided your family's dairy products, including milk, cheese, and eggs. Unless you're buying "organic" or "free-range" dairy products, you're probably purchasing food from animals who suffered. Blessing these animals can help you minimize the dairy products' energy of pain so that your family doesn't ingest the negativity.

Whenever you eat at a restaurant, you may unknowingly absorb the energy of the cooks, waiters, and food preparers. If any of these workers are holding angry thoughts, your food's life-force energy may be affected. For that reason, it's best to hold your hands over your plate of food prior to eating it. Visualize white-light energy coming from your hands, surrounding the food. Say a prayer, asking that the energy of love be absorbed into the food.

Scott McGuffey, a spiritual counselor and friend of ours, had a dramatic experience with the power that blessings have upon the life-force energy of food. Here's how Scott describes it:

"I went to a natural food store and deli to get lunch. As I stepped up to the counter to have my order taken, I noticed that the woman behind the counter who was going to make my sandwich was very agitated. She was complaining under her breath about how understaffed they were. I wondered if her fear energy would affect my food. I heard my guardian angel say that it was okay to get the sandwich.

"The sandwich was made very poorly. Although I ordered organic veggies on multigrain bread, the sandwich looked sick. Before I could take a bite, my angel told me to cut the sandwich in half, and then in half again.

"She then instructed me to take one quarter of the sandwich and wrap it up. For the other quarter, the angel told me to hold my hands over the sandwich and ask that it be blessed and cleansed with white light, and then wrap it up. I was guided to keep it separate from the 'untouched' piece. I was then asked to bless the remaining half and eat it!

"When I got back to my office 20 minutes later, I put the two quarters of the sandwich in the refrigerator so that I would have something to eat for dinner. About four and a half hours passed, and I went back to the refrigerator and retrieved my two quarters.

"I unwrapped them side by side, and the difference was unbelievable. The 'untouched' one looked like it had been sitting in the fridge for about a week. It was soggy, and looked brown and aged. The veggies were lifeless and wilted.

"In complete contrast, though, the blessed piece of sandwich looked very healthy and alive! It was not soggy, nor was it brown. The difference was really amazing. Now, whenever I eat out, I say a prayer over my food, especially when I can't see who has prepared it."

Organics Are Your Friend

As vegans, we consume larger amounts of fruits and vegetables than meat-eaters. So it's doubly important for vegans to choose organic versions of their foods and vegetables to avoid consuming toxic pesticides and herbicides. After all, anything that is meant to kill insects will also harm other organisms.

Most organic farms are small and labors-of-love by farmers who believe in organic sustainable farming. They work directly with the soil and tend to their plants with loving care. Of course their fruits and vegetables are going to taste better!

Studies show that organic produce contains significantly higher levels of vitamins and minerals. And two studies reported significantly lower urinary pesticide levels among children with organic versus conventional diets.

Subjectively, most agree that it tastes much better than factory-farmed produce, which is picked while unripe and sprayed or trucked to ripen.

Another reason to eat organic is to avoid consuming or financing genetically modified organisms (GMOs, sometimes called GE). GMO products have insect-killing toxins genetically built into their seeds and structure. So insects and worms that eat GMO foods die. But why would we believe this is safe for any other organism (such as us humans) to consume?

Manufacturers of GMO seeds spend millions of dollars annually trying to convince consumers and politicians that their lucrative products are safe and that organics don't have benefits. Don't believe their propaganda! Steer far away from anything GMO for the health of yourself and your planet.

As of the publication of this book, these foods are most likely GMO unless you buy or grow certified-organic or heirloom varieties:

Top Genetically Modified Foods—
Avoid Unless They're Certified Organic

Potatoes

Corn
(including corn syrup,
corn powder)

Beets
(including beet sugar)

Rice

Soy products
(including soybean oil)

Squash

Wheat

Hawaiian papayas

Tomatoes

Yeast

Bananas

Honey
(bees feed off GMO canola,
and most honey is adulter-
ated with GMO corn syrup)

Salmon

Aspartame
(NutraSweet)

Cotton
(and cottonseed oil)

Canola oil

Peas

Meat, eggs, and dairy
products*

*Cows and chickens are fed GMO feed and are given growth hor-
mones, antibiotics, and other additives that enter their milk and
flesh; in addition, if an animal suffered during its life or slaughter, its
by-products are filled with pain energy, which transfers to whoever
consumes these items.

Some countries have banned GMO production or
require labeling on product ingredient lists. Our prayer

is that GMO is banned worldwide in the near future. In the meantime, do protect your health by purchasing certified-organic versions of the products listed on the previous page.

You can find inexpensive organics at farmers' markets, local co-ops, and small non-chain health-food stores. Even better, buy heirloom seeds and start your own organic non-GMO garden!

A Note about Soy

Since so many vegans and vegetarians rely upon plant-based proteins and meat substitutes, it's important for us to discuss soy.

As mentioned previously, soy is among the most commonly grown genetically modified food. It's estimated that 93 percent of the world's soybeans are GMO.

In addition, some people are sensitive to the estrogen-producing effect of soy and soy products (tofu, soy milk, soy margarine, soybean oil, and so on). Some women must avoid soy and estrogen for their health.

If you do choose to consume soy products, it's essential that you verify that it's certified organic. If you live in a country with mandatory GMO-labeling laws, read the ingredients list carefully. Before eating tofu at a restaurant, ask if it's organic.

The Physical Impact of Food

Fatigue and foggy thinking can stem from lack of sleep, increased stress, illness, inactivity, lack of fluid intake, too much or too little food, and eating food that doesn't agree with you. Have you ever gone several hours without eating, only to find yourself shaky, in a cold sweat, irritable, and grabbing for the first thing at hand? Usually you'll end up craving and eating a sweet treat.

Your body knows that your blood sugar is low and needs to be raised. This condition, known as hypoglycemia, occurs whenever your food intake is inadequate. For those with the medical diagnosis of hypoglycemia, low blood sugar may occur every two to three hours. Others can go for four to six hours without noticing a drop in their blood sugar.

Eating well has a domino effect. For example, you may find that when your health improves, so does your mood. You have more energy to do meaningful activities, which opens the door to your creativity, which then increases your energy.

Food can be broken down into three components: carbohydrates, proteins, and fats. Each of these components provides energy or fuel. Of the three, carbohydrates and proteins are broken down further into glucose (blood sugar). You use this energy to perform physical activities such as jogging up a hill; intellectual activities such as solving a problem; or emotional activities such as bursting out with a big belly laugh.

Our brain functions solely on glucose. Your ability to read this book stems largely from the fact that you have enough glucose floating around in your brain to fuel an understanding of words and sentences. The same is true with physical activity. You can run, swim, bike, and hike because you have energy reserves of glucose in your liver and muscles, called glycogen. Without it, you couldn't complete various physical and mental activities.

A major concern of those who adopt a vegetarian diet is, "Will I get enough protein?" As you'll read in the next chapter, a plant-based diet provides more than adequate protein levels. As such, your vegan diet will ensure that you have ready supplies of life-force energy, meaning that you'll feel healthy and vigorous as a result.

The Emotional Impact of Food

Many people adopt spiritual practices and principles in the search for peace and happiness, and it's true that your diet can definitely impact your emotions and state of mind. The link between food and mood has been established by hundreds of scientific studies. Many of these studies show that depression, anxiety, lethargy, and cravings can result from a poor or imbalanced diet.

Cravings for food are a sign that the body and the emotions are looking for peace or homeostasis. Cravings can mean that some vitamin or mineral is depleted in the body. However, they can also stem from emotional imbalances. Whenever there are imbalances, we receive guidance (in the form of gut feelings, ideas, visions, or an inner voice) to change the situation causing the imbalance. However, if we ignore this guidance, the body pressures us to regain homeostasis in a different way, such as through craving certain foods. Intuitively, the body knows that certain foods will alter the brain chemicals or blood pressure in order to regulate energy or mood.

For example, let's say that you're unhappy at work. You feel pressured to perform the job of three employees without receiving adequate pay or approval. After a while, you begin to feel burned-out, so your inner guidance pressures you to make a life change. Perhaps you get a feeling that you should brush up your résumé and contact an employment agency.

Unfortunately, your fears about financial security or about change in general keep you from following this guidance.

So your body then sends you signals to eat certain foods that will help you temporarily feel better. Each food is craved because it has amino acids, neurochemical catalysts, or vasoconstrictor catalysts, which will energize your body or soothe your brain chemicals. Here are some common cravings associated with specific life situations:

Food Craved	Effect	Life Situation
Red meat	Stimulating	Burnout, usually from work
Fatty foods	Soothing	Financial insecurity
Sharp cheese	Stimulating	Fatigue—pushing oneself to work, rushing too much
Vanilla ice cream	Soothing	Tension, fear, depression

To deal with food cravings, first make sure that your body is physically fulfilled. This may mean taking a multivitamin each day (check the label to make sure it says "Suitable for Vegetarians," since some vitamins have beef, fish, egg, or other animal by-product ingredients). My (Doreen's) book *Constant Craving* lists hundreds of food cravings and their underlying meanings.

Your emotions also require adequate supplies of a brain chemical called "serotonin." Without sufficient serotonin, you may feel tired, depressed, irritable, or have cravings for carbohydrates. Some natural ways to increase your serotonin supply include the following:

- Engaging in aerobic activities (running, fast walking, stair-climbing, etc.) for at least 20 minutes, four or five times a week

- Being outside in the sunlight

- Avoiding or reducing alcohol and caffeine consumption, which inhibit serotonin production

- Touching a loved one, and being touched

- Eating a balanced diet, with plenty of whole grains and fresh produce

- Sleeping soundly for at least seven hours a night (if you are male) or eight hours (if you are female), without the use of sleep-enhancers (that is, alcohol, downers, etc.)

Once your body is taken care of, any additional food cravings you experience will probably have an emotional basis. The most direct route to reducing cravings is to heal the situation that's triggering them. Even taking a baby step toward the resolution of a problem at work, in your love life, or in your lifestyle can reduce food cravings.

Affirmations are another powerful solution to handling food cravings. Begin each day by affirming:

🖎 *I crave healthful foods.*

🖎 *I love exercising.*

🖎 *My body is fit and healthy.*

🖎 *I can easily afford to buy organic food.*

🖎 *I have plenty of time for exercise.*

🖎 *I love eating fresh fruits and vegetables.*

🖎 *When I eat healthfully, I feel wonderful.*

Then, throughout the day, fill your mind with positive affirmations about the situation that seems to be triggering your food cravings. For instance, if you're craving steak or bacon to increase your energy at a job that you don't like, you can say affirmations to motivate you to make changes. These might include, *My work is meaningful and fulfilling,* or *I am open to making positive changes in my life.*

If your cravings seem more geared toward high-fat foods, you're most likely feeling some insecurity that you're trying to fill with fat. Fat stays in the stomach long after other forms of food have been digested and emptied. So, fat cravings often occur in people who feel that their life lacks meaning, who feel empty, or who feel financially or emotionally insecure.

Some affirmations for these situations include those to increase your abundance, such as: *Waves of abundance are flowing through me right now;* affirmations to add meaning to your life, such as: *New opportunities to make the world a better place are now open to me;* and affirmations to add self-confidence, such as: *I am valuable and lovable just for being who I am.*

You can also ask God and your guardian angels to help you with food cravings. Many of my students report that their prayers for relief from cravings are answered. Additionally, Angel Therapy is a powerful way to clear, or reduce, food cravings.

To perform angel therapy on yourself, mentally ask Archangel Michael (who clears away the residue of fear) and Archangel Raphael (the healing angel) to enter into your mind, heart, and body. Depending upon your spiritual orientation, you may also want to invite in God, the Holy Spirit, Jesus, Mary, or your guides.

Mentally say to your helpers, *I am willing to release the fears that are triggering my food cravings. Please clear away the effects of fear from my thoughts, my cellular memory, my heart, and my body.* Then, let the angels do the rest of the work, while you simply stay open to their help. Watch for any tendency to hold your breath while the angels are working. When we breathe, we open the door to spiritual healing.

You can ask for this angelic help as often as you like. It's especially powerful to invite in this healing right before you go to bed. While you're sleeping, your skeptical mind is also asleep, making you more open to receiving spiritual assistance. (For more details about this subject, refer to *Constant Craving*.)

Food and Spirituality

Different foods have varying effects on our chakra energy system. They can support, hinder, or be neutral to it. Dense foods (with a low life-force energy) tend to close the chakras, while light foods (with higher life-force energy levels) tend to open them. For example, meats that have a low life-force energy have a chakra-closing effect. A fresh fruit salad, in contrast, can help chakras become larger and brighter.

Why do so many spiritual masters and organizations praise the benefits of a vegetarian diet for their devotees? One stage of progression along the path of self-discovery might be called the "purification stage." Paying close attention to the energy levels of foods that you eat has the most profound effect during this stage.

There are enlightened masters, yogis, and others who aren't affected at all by what they eat. Some have even ingested lethal doses of pharmaceuticals without any effect. These individuals are on a higher vibrational level than most of the populace. But, along their path to get to this level, most of these mystics went through a vegetarian and purification stage in their development. In the same manner, the ancient Greek philosopher and mathematician Pythagoras had the students in his mystery school adopt a vegan diet.

Doreen's Story

"When I began devoting my private practice to conducting spiritual counseling, I asked for Divine guidance on how to increase my clairvoyance. I immediately saw, in my mind's eye, an image of chicken meat pieces. I figured that my guides misunderstood my question, so I asked again, 'What steps can I take to increase the vividness of my clairvoyance?' Again, I saw a mental picture of raw chicken meat.

"This made no sense to me, so I asked my guides to clarify what they meant by this image. Immediately, I heard them say, 'You are blocking your clairvoyance by eating chicken, since you are absorbing the energy of pain when you eat it.' This seemed bizarre, almost unbelievable to me, so I asked a more experienced clairvoyant for confirmation of my Divine guidance. He validated that many people who are interested in developing their psychic abilities are guided to drop meat from their diets.

"Since that time, I have adopted a vegan diet, which means that I don't eat any animal products. My clairvoyance has dramatically improved, and I feel wonderful.

"At my workshops, I help audience members hear the voice of their angels. One of the questions that they ask their angels is, 'How can I improve my ability to see and hear you?' About half the time, the angels say, 'You're eating too much cheese (or milk, or some other dairy product).' The angels explain that dairy products clog the psychic senses. Excessive dairy shows up in the aura, looking like a milky cloud surrounding the person, with a greasy feel to it.

"Since animal products contain a low life-force energy, they slow the chakras. Increased psychic and intuitive abilities are one of the many benefits of adopting a vegan diet."

CHAPTER THREE

Making the Transition

"One is dearest to God who has no enemies among the living beings, who is nonviolent to all creatures."
— FROM THE BHAGAVAD GITA

Life seems to constantly present us with changing scenery. In fact, change may be the only constant part of life! The more we embrace and welcome change, the easier and smoother our transitions become. When we make a change because of love, the change is usually lasting. However, when fear motivates us to change, the change is usually short-lived.

Making dietary changes is no different. If you decide to become a vegan for loving reasons, such as loving your body, your spiritual gifts, animals, and the environment, you'll enjoy the transition more. However, if you are motivated by fear—such as wanting to lose weight to please someone else—you're apt to struggle with food cravings and dissatisfaction.

One simple way of modeling a life change is by using the "ADA 3-Step Process":

- A is for **Awareness**

- D is for **Decision**

- A is for **Action**

Step 1: Awareness. Awareness means that you have a conscious awareness of the issue, or your reasons for desiring a change. Upon becoming aware, you can then make a . . .

Step 2: Decision. Making a decision is making a choice, to do or not to do, after which . . .

Step 3: Action comes into play. Action incorporates your follow-through. It's important to associate Step 1 as much as possible with Step 3 so that change can occur, with the realization that a personal decision

(Step 2) has been made. This is opposed to being *pressured* into a change, which usually leads to resentment.

Sometimes Step 2 (Decision) can cause people to get stuck, and then confusion sets in. Change involves risk. Knowing the degree to which you are willing to change assists in the change process and helps to keep you open. As mentioned earlier, though, sometimes people get stuck while trying to make a decision. Time passes, and ultimately no decision is made, which is actually a decision in itself.

Human behavior usually causes us to take the easiest choice when we have alternatives available to us. So, it's easier to procrastinate, keep living a sedentary lifestyle, or continue eating fatty animal foods than to change. Here are some ways to motivate yourself if you become stuck in this way:

— **Make a list of pros and cons.** Write down the benefits and drawbacks of becoming a vegan. If you note more pros than cons, keep reviewing the list each time you feel unsure of your decision.

— **Test-drive your future.** Imagine how your body, health, energy level, relationships, and career will be affected if you become a vegan. Then, imagine the alternative. How will your future look if you continue with your present lifestyle?

— **Ask your gut.** Go within and ask your inner self, *How do you feel about becoming a vegan?* Then, pay attention to any changes in your gut feelings. Does it tighten? Become lighter and brighter? Do you seem to get a positive or negative reaction from your gut? Mentally interview your gut, and ask it, *Why do you feel that way?* and *What do you want?* Your gut feelings will guide you to honestly listen to your soul's needs, instead of your body's Earthly desires.

— **Watch out for all-or-nothing mental traps.** Sometimes we resist making changes because they feel too overwhelming. If you're balking at veganism, perhaps it's because you need to make the transition gradually. For instance, begin with one vegan meal a week. Then, make two meals a week vegan, and so on. This also gives your stomach a chance to adapt to a lower-fat diet so that you won't feel hungry from going "cold turkey" from meat (no pun intended!).

For most of us, small changes work best over the long haul. A concrete plan of action, such as "avoiding red meat" or "every Wednesday, I'll eat a plant-based dinner," is especially helpful when we're first beginning a change. Small, concrete plans help to support new routines, which serve a purpose. They help to organize us; and make us feel comfortable, safe, and warm.

So, when you embrace change at first, you can expect to feel disorganized and a little uncomfortable. Establishing a routine, which you can continue to modify throughout your life, will support you in your desire to change. Here are some steps you might take when making your transition to veganism. You can perform these steps in whatever time frame seems natural and comfortable to you.

Ten Suggested Steps for Making the Switch to Veganism

1. **Adopt a meditation program,** such as yoga, *A Course in Miracles,* or sitting quietly with your eyes shut. Notice your breathing, thoughts, and emotions. Be aware of how your body feels, and any messages it seems to be signaling to you. Keep a journal of any insights.

2. **Become aware of how you feel when you eat.** Eat one food at a time so you will clearly

see how that particular food affects you.
Record the feelings and reactions you get for
each food in your journal.

3. **Note how you feel when you eat meat,
and how you feel afterward.** Record these
feelings—without editing, judging, or censor-
ing them—in your journal.

4. **See how you feel when eating or drinking
dairy products.**

5. **Purchase or borrow some vegetarian magazines and books** to get new recipes and ideas
for meat substitutes as you prepare to become
a vegan.

6. **Eliminate beef and pork from your diet.**

7. **Eliminate dairy products.**

8. **Eliminate chicken and turkey.**

9. **Eliminate eggs.**

10. **Eliminate fish.**

The goal is for you to achieve success while being
flexible and compassionate with yourself. For instance,
you may want to transpose Steps 7 and 8. Remember,
the goal is a process, not a destination. As you begin

to change, this modification will have a rippling effect on you and those around you, with the ripples eventually reaching everyone. Your friends and family will either embrace these movements, or show resistance and rejection. Honoring people's process of change is important.

Gradually Becoming Vegan

Our attitude permeates everything, including when we make changes. Attitude places a lens on how we view and embrace life. If we think something is helpful, then it will be. Is love or fear your filter in life? Energetically, love leaves us open, while fear spins us off-center and ultimately shuts us down. Are you a vegan because this is a loving act for your body and the environment, or is it out of fear that you may have a heart attack as a result of a fatty diet? Love always heals fear and creates more love, while fear only creates more fear.

The most common reason why people switch to veganism is to gain a greater feeling of well-being. This well-being is experienced as having more energy, thinking more clearly, and having a greater connectedness to animal and plant life. Weight loss is a possible side benefit of becoming a vegan.

Awareness, decision-making, and action (the ADA of change) may look different for each of us. Gradual change invites others to join us. When we go down the river too fast, we may leave our loved ones on the river bank, with no bridge to connect us. Honor the changeability in others, especially when it shows up in a different way from what you regard as right or appropriate. That is why changing for oneself, and not to please others, is so important. If others come along for the journey, that's great; otherwise, move on with a smile.

Having a plan and developing a routine helps to establish a foundation. From this foundation, you can build a bridge to reach your family and friends. Slowly introducing new food items to your loved ones is one way to invite them to step on to your bridge to meet you.

Your bridge can be constructed with some of the old, while incorporating the new. Making meatloaf illustrates how you can do this. At first, you can make it with your usual recipe, using a meat source and adding a little organic tofu, seitan, or other organic meat substitutes. Over time, you can replace a major quantity of the meat with vegan ingredients. Eventually, your meatloaf will become a vegan or vegetarian loaf.

When we first improve our diet, we usually reduce or eliminate junk food, caffeine, and sugared snacks from our meals. When we hear people talk about eating a plant-based diet, they usually describe how energetic they feel as a result. This makes sense, since most Americans eat two to four times the amount of animal protein that they need, which can led to fatigue. Animal-based protein has a nitrogen atom on it. This nitrogen needs to be processed with water so it can be released from the body as urea.

Most people do not drink enough water. Water needs are increased when we eat animal products. When we don't drink enough water, fatigue is the end result. When we are even one percent dehydrated, we become fatigued. Once animal protein is decreased in the diet, the water needs reduce, and fatigue is less likely.

An inviting way to use the imagination is to remove all the rules, listen to your feelings, and inject your own creativity into your meal-making. You may find it helpful to follow a recipe once or twice, in order to be aware of one possible way the recipe can taste. Once you gain confidence, you'll feel open to adding your own touches. This openness to add an artistic license to someone else's recipe allows a flow to occur, which supports and inspires your creative energy.

Tips for Those Who Resist Vegan Meals

Lisa Tracy wrote a book called *The Gradual Vegetarian,* in which she endorses making *lifestyle* changes versus following a *diet.* "Diet" actually means what we eat, but the popular definition of the word *diet* is shrouded with ideas of restrictions. If we switch overnight to a vegan diet, we may feel restricted and controlled.

Most people can tolerate feeling restricted for a certain amount of time, and then they rebel because they feel deprived. They eventually swing back in the direction they just left. However, slow, bite-sized changes will ensure success.

It's not that difficult to simultaneously fix a vegan meal for yourself and a meat-based meal for your family members. Get out two frying or baking pans and cook fish filets or chicken for the family, and make a vegetable burger for yourself, then make the side dishes vegan or vegetarian. Some examples of vegan side dishes include: rice pilaf made with coconut oil, a tossed green salad, baked organic potatoes, gluten-free pasta with olive oil or marinara sauce, steamed vegetables, bean salad, vegetable soup, or gluten-free muffins. Everyone in the family—whether vegan or not—can enjoy these dishes together.

Here are some ways to reframe how you and your family may view veganism:

— **Notice which meals your family enjoys that are already vegetarian.** For instance, spaghetti with marinara sauce, grilled-cheese sandwiches, macaroni and cheese, or bean burritos.

— **Revise your favorite meat-based recipes to make them vegetarian.** Start with the easy ones. Replace the meat in chili, spaghetti, tacos, or lasagna with a meat substitute such as:

- *Organic tofu.* Tofu easily absorbs the flavor of sauces. Soft tofu "crumbles" like ground meat. Firm or super-firm tofu cuts nicely into cubes. Or, purchase prebaked and marinated tofu, which is highly flavorful. It's essential that you only buy and eat organic non–genetically modified tofu, to avoid ingesting chemicals. Additionally, some people are sensitive to the estrogen effects of soy, as mentioned previously, and cannot tolerate soy in any form.

- *TVP (textured vegetable protein).* This is available in freeze-dried form, in boxes, in the deli, or in the freezer in a flavored form. Hamburger- and sausage-like TVP is available in plastic tubes, in the deli section of health-food stores. If you are gluten-intolerant, be sure to read the ingredients to look for wheat.

Tempeh. This product, made from fermented soybeans, is chewier than meat, and doesn't really taste like meat. However, it does provide good taste and bulk in dishes that normally call for ground meat. As with any soy product, it's essential that you buy only organic, non-GMO varieties, and know your health tolerance for the estrogen effect of soy.

Seitan or wheat-meat. Available in chicken or beef-flavored varieties in the deli section of health-food stores, seitan (also known as wheat-meat) has a satisfying taste and a chewy texture. It can be cut into strips, to substitute for stroganoff or fajita recipes. Those who are gluten-intolerant may have an inflammation effect from eating any wheat products.

— **Skip the breakfast meat**, or substitute organic-soy-based bacon or sausage-like products, which are available in the freezer section of most grocery or health-food stores.

— **Try smoothies**. Children, teens, and adults alike find smoothies a wonderful meal supplement or substitute. You can add vitamin, fiber, and protein supplements to the smoothie to help finicky eaters fulfill their nutritional needs.

— **Introduce beans gradually into your meals.** Add some to your salad, a rice dish, or your soup. Beans create bulk, fiber, and healthful protein. They also absorb the flavors of spices and sauces.

— **Base your food intake on plant foods.** Too much dairy in the form of milk, cheese, or yogurt may raise the fat content, while leaving less appetite for fiber-rich foods. Limit the use of dairy foods to no more than one meal a day. Use hummus (a dip made of ground beans, available in the deli section of most grocery or health-food stores, or make your own) as a substitute for cheese or sour cream.

— **Remember that grains, vegetables, beans, and nuts all provide protein.** Vegans do not need to eat special combinations of foods at one meal to meet protein needs. As long as calorie needs are sufficient and you eat a variety of foods, protein needs are easily met. Kale, for example, is extremely high in protein.

— **Be patient with the finicky eater in your family.** Start with easy foods to invite them in (meatless spaghetti, lasagna, stir-fry, etc.). Don't insist that they eat the more unusual foods. Be loving, hold your position, and as much as possible, let the fussy eaters fend for themselves.

Building a Strong Bridge

Commitment, clarity, compassion, and creativity all help to build a strong bridge. Form a definite image of the type of vegetarian you'd like to become. Become clear on how feasible this is. Are other people involved? Do you have the time to prepare your meals? Be compassionate with yourself. As you visualize yourself learning new vegan cooking skills, love and encouragement is what you need, not personal criticism. Become creative in your life in all ways, including how you cook and eat.

Planning will support the commitment you choose to make in switching from a meat-based diet to a plant-based one. Keeping the changes simple will help you maintain your clarity. Consciously coming from a space of love and care will build compassion. Giving yourself permission to use your imagination will provide a continual spark to your creativity.

An integral part of planning is to have a shopping list, and avoid going to the store when you're hungry. Create the list from the recipes you're going to make in the next three to five days. Shopping while your stomach is full will minimize impulse buying. Both a shopping list and a full tummy will keep you on track and help you solidify your commitment to a vegan diet.

Clarity also means keeping things simple. For example, it's frustrating to be out of shape, and then you go back to the gym for the first time and overdo it. Your muscles are so sore that you momentarily wonder what happened to your body, until you recall your enthusiastic return to the gym. The same is true with food. You want to make sure you don't bite off more than you can chew—literally and figuratively.

Choose new recipes that are in your ballpark. If you're not accustomed to cooking, select a simple recipe that you'll be successful at making, versus a gourmet recipe that may leave you crying with frustration. A peanut-butter-and-jelly sandwich made with love and care will hold that compassion. When consumed by you, you will *digest* that compassion. If the food is not made with love but you bless and adore it, the food will be transformed, and you will be, too.

𝒟 𝒟 𝒟

CHAPTER FOUR

Vegan Myths Debunked

*"A good deed done to an animal is as
meritorious as a good deed done to a human being,
while an act of cruelty to an animal is as bad as
an act of cruelty to a human being."*

— MOHAMMED, FOUNDER OF ISLAM

Part of your successful transition to a vegan lifestyle depends on how comfortable you feel about
adopting a plant-based diet. Sometimes people are
afraid to stop eating meat because they believe some
of the myths about being a vegan. Becoming informed

about the truth of veganism can help you let go of any fears you may have that stem from these untruths.

Here are the seven most common misconceptions about veganism, along with the facts to dispel them:

Seven Vegan Myths

1. "I will not get enough protein in my diet."

2. "Animal protein is superior to plant protein."

3. "Being a vegan means only eating salads."

4. "I will lose muscle mass if I'm a vegan."

5. "It's difficult to be a vegan."

6. "Being a vegan is time-consuming."

7. "Eating organic is expensive."

Myth: I will not get enough protein in my diet.

Truth: Many people eat two to four times the amount of protein that they need.

Many people in America were raised with the fear of protein malnourishment if they didn't eat meat every day. Most of us remember our grade-school teachers pointing to large posters showing red meat, and urging us to eat from the four food groups (meat, dairy, grain, and fruits and vegetables) daily. What our teachers didn't show us was the backside of those posters, which revealed the names of the cattle and dairy businesses and councils who paid for the posters' printing and distribution.

As a result of these inaccurate lessons, today most Americans overconsume animal protein. A comprehensive study done in China by Cornell University showed a link between the consumption of animal sources of protein and an increased occurrence of osteoporosis. Many of these studies are featured in the classic book *The China Study* by T. Colin Campbell. It's probably no coincidence that so many people consume animal protein daily, at the same time that osteoporosis is practically at epidemic proportions.

A high-protein diet has been advocated by several popular books, including *Dr. Atkins' New Diet Revolution, The Zone,* and *Eat Right for Your Type.* However, as we mentioned earlier, a high-protein diet requires a large consumption of water, which is needed to help digest protein. When we don't drink enough water, we experience dehydration. With just one percent dehydration, the first symptom is fatigue. Many people are tired because their excess protein intake is dehydrating them.

Myth: Animal protein is superior to plant protein.

Truth: All food sources, except fat and sugar, have protein in them.

"The Food Pyramid" is a nutritional recommendation system that breaks foods into different groups and provides serving numbers and sizes. Using this Food Pyramid as a basis, here are the approximate protein contents of different vegan and non-vegan foods per serving:

- ✐ **The bread group** has 3 grams of protein (i.e., 1 slice bread or ½ cup rice)

- ✐ **The vegetable group** has 2 grams of protein (i.e., ½ cup cooked or 1 cup raw)

- ✐ **The fruit group** has a half gram of protein (i.e., 1 piece or ½ cup juice)

- ✐ **The milk group** has 8 grams of protein (i.e., 1 cup milk or yogurt)

- ✐ **The meat group** has 7 grams per ounce (i.e., 3 oz.)

Myth: Being a vegan means only eating salads.

Truth: You *could* eat only salads as a vegan, but why would you do that to yourself when there are so many vegan eating options?

Any dish can be re-created from plant-based ingredients, including ethnic dishes, baked goods, traditional breakfast meals, holiday dishes, desserts, and so forth. The high-quality meat substitutes available at health-food stores and vegan restaurants are virtually indistinguishable from animal products. There are vegan versions of all traditional cooking and baking ingredients, and you can use these substitutes in traditional recipes.

Myth: I will lose muscle mass if I'm a vegan.

Truth: Eating complex carbohydrates, along with doing challenging workouts with weights, stimulates muscle growth.

Contrary to popular belief, one does not need to consume a lot of extra protein to build muscle mass. The confusion has to do with the role that proteins play in our body. The job of protein is to build and repair. Some people think that "building and repairing" equates to bigger biceps. However, protein performs several building tasks. It builds red and white blood cells, and all enzymes and hormones. Every cell in our body has protein in its membrane; and our skin, hair, and nails are made up of protein, as are our organs.

In addition, our skin sloughs off every 30 days and needs to be replaced, and the cells inside of our mouth are released every three days. A red blood cell has a life span of 120 days. All of this is to say that the body makes a lot of things from the protein we eat; however, building muscle mass is not at the top of the list.

Myth: It's difficult to be a vegan.

Truth: As with anything new, you may feel a little awkward at the beginning of your dietary changes.

However, if you approach the changes by regarding them as an adventure that has far-reaching benefits, you may be more willing to face any challenge.

You can make your eating transition easier by developing a meal plan, buying vegan cookbooks, being more organized while shopping for food, eating at vegetarian restaurants, and by gradually incorporating veganism into your life.

With time, you'll learn how to order vegan food at any restaurant and how to harmoniously eat at friends' dinner parties, while maintaining your vegan lifestyle. Have patience with yourself while you incorporate this significant change into your life. Your self-esteem will rise with each success that you have.

If your family presents difficulties, do your best to be patient. Start with basic vegan foods, such as meatless spaghetti, lasagna, chili, or tostadas. Don't push the more exotic vegan meals on your family members. Be loving, but stand your ground.

Myth: Being a vegan is time-consuming.

Truth: Breaking old shopping, cooking, and eating habits is the most time-consuming part of becoming vegan.

Most of us are creatures of habit, so you may feel confused at first about what to cook for dinner, or what ingredients to buy at the store.

You may need to change where you shop, so try to scout out a good health-food store. Fortunately, we now live in a time when large health-food grocery stores are plentiful. Many of the major outlets have websites where you can purchase groceries online and have them delivered to your home. Freeze-dried meat substitutes and healthy seasonings are just a couple of the types of items that you can buy from your home computer. You'll find many of these website addresses in the Resources section of this book.

Cooking meat actually takes more time than vegan cooking. After all, you need to ensure that the meat is cooked thoroughly to avoid food poisoning. The reverse is true with vegan meal preparation. If you're cooking vegetables, for example, the less you cook them, the more healthful they are to eat. Most meat substitutes are precooked, or require little more than sautéing or warming. Seasoning and sauces are key ingredients that make for delicious vegan meals. Since you can purchase premade sauces and pre-chopped vegetables, it's possible to shop and dine very quickly as a vegan.

When trying any new recipe, it's normal to feel awkward or confused at first. Many find that they must make a new recipe three times before they begin to feel comfortable. By the fourth time, they've got the recipe memorized and begin to experiment with the ingredients.

Myth: Eating organic is expensive.

Truth: If you shop at farmers' markets, co-ops, or local farms, or grow your own, organic prices are comparable to pesticide-sprayed produce. Besides, with the health dangers of non-organic, you'll pay for eating the toxic chemicals in other ways.

Everyone, whether vegan or not, should do their best to eat as much organic non–genetically modified food as possible. As a vegan who is health-conscious, you'll want to ensure that your fruits, vegetables, and grains are organic.

However, there's a myth that organic foods are too expensive for the average consumer's budget. While some organic markets do charge more than the discount stores, prices are leveling as more consumers demand organic food choices. If your local market doesn't carry organic produce and other supplies, ask the manager to order them . . . and then be sure to buy the items to encourage the store to continue stocking them.

Farmers' markets, local farms, co-ops, and your own garden are the least expensive way to purchase fruits and vegetables. Plus, you have the added ecological, community, and energy benefits of shopping and eating locally grown food!

A Low-Key Approach

Family celebrations, birthdays, holidays, ordering at restaurants, eating at friends' houses, and entertaining others are just a few events and situations that revolve around food. If you feel strongly about your new vegan lifestyle, the best way to convey this message to others is by example, rather than by lecturing them.

Many people are turned off by overly vigilant vegans. We've all met many "warrior" vegans, who seem to have a sense of righteousness. And even though there are many wonderful reasons why people become vegan, thinking that you're superior to others is not a valid one.

After all, who likes to be pushed into anything? Remember that time when you were interested in buying something, but you never went through with it because an overly zealous salesperson made you run in the opposite direction? Well, think about how *you* prefer to learn about something that you have reservations about.

The goal is to be mindful of not coercing your friends and family into a vegan lifestyle. What usually happens is that one member of the family, often the cook, discovers vegan eating and the benefits that can go along with it. Then this person is eager to have everyone join in. That course of action works for some people, but most prefer a low-key approach, which opens up their receptivity to new—and sometimes unusual—food.

So, putting a single animal-rights bumper sticker on your car is one thing (multiple stickers make you look like a zealot, causing others to dismiss you altogether), but lecturing your family about the gory details of animal slaughter is another. Your friends and family will notice that you don't eat meat, and if they're interested in veganism, they will ask you about it. Even then, don't be overly forceful or strident with your answers. A simple, calm answer to the question, "Why are you a vegan?" can be much more effective than a defensive one.

The Skeptical and the Concerned

"Aren't you afraid that you won't get enough protein from your vegan diet?" your well-meaning Aunt Edna asks you. Education, thoughtfulness, and commitment are three ingredients that will help you deal with your skeptical and overly concerned loved ones.

The more educated and centered you are about veganism, the more your family and friends will be at ease. Reading books about veganism, or the magazine *Vegetarian Times*, will give you additional information to discuss with others. It's best to avoid debating the pros and cons of veganism. Simply teach through example. If your vegan lifestyle has helped you become more peaceful, healthful, and happy, other individuals will definitely take notice.

The most common question that your loved ones will probably pose has to do with necessary amounts of protein and calories. Share with them that you plan to eat foods that are complementary, and that these foods have the amino-acid profile of a steak. This will greatly lessen their concerns.

For those raised in cultures centered around meat in meals, the idea of not eating meat seems disrespectful. In America, for example, we grew up with images of burgers, shakes, fries, and apple pie. This image is and has been an intrinsic part of our pop culture. How many 1950s movies have you seen with the classic burger stand backdrop? And doesn't "fine dining" mean filet mignon, rack of lamb, or a swordfish steak?

The world is slowly rewriting its beliefs about healthful eating. Many burger stands now offer vegiburgers, and supermarkets have vegan selections and organic produce. Your loved ones have most likely noticed these changes, too.

How Do You Handle Children Who Wrinkle Their Noses?

If you want to introduce your kids to vegan food, it's best to do so gradually. For example, cook and serve regular hot dogs and organic tofu hot dogs together. When serving milk, mix ¼ glass of almond or organic rice milk with the dairy milk. Be a role model by "ooh-ing" and "aahing" while eating your vegan foods.

If you or your children are newcomers to health-ful eating, it's important to know that your desire for junk food or processed food may continue for a few months. But just be persistent. After one or two months, the cravings for salt, sugar, and fat will likely be replaced with the desire for wholesome foods.

You can help the situation by clearing your cup-boards and refrigerator of candy and junk food. Have plenty of healthful "finger foods" readily available, such as a bowl of organic grapes, ripe strawberries, melon slices, hummus dip with broccoli florets, trail mix, or whole-grain crackers.

Here are some other ideas for vegan meals and snacks for your children.

Vegan Snacks and Meals That Offer Children Complementary Proteins

- Rice pudding made with almond milk
- A bagel with almond butter, sunflower butter, or tahini
- Hummus in pita bread

- A bean burrito with pinto beans in a flour tortilla

- A veggie burger taco with an organic corn tortilla

- Soup with barley, organic brown rice, and kale

- Soup with macaroni and beans

Vegan Ideas for Quick and Portable Snacks and Meals for Teenagers

- Dried fruit

- Trail mix

- Popcorn

- Rice cakes

- Organic nondairy yogurt

- Leftover pizza or frozen pizza slices

- Smoothies

- Hummus in pita bread

- A muffin and juice

- A bagel with peanut butter

- A peanut butter-and-banana sandwich

- Almond butter on crackers

When Friends Invite You Over for Dinner

It's fun to have dinner at a friend's home, and just because you're a vegan or vegetarian, it doesn't mean that you have to forsake the fun associated with eating delicious food. You can approach this situation in different ways. You'll just need to consult your inner guide to decide which method works best for you.

Doreen's Story

"I use humor in these situations. It seems to break any tension that could arise because of my vegan lifestyle. When someone invites me to dinner at their home, I usually answer, 'Are you sure you want me over? After all, I'm a vegan. You know—those people who don't eat any meat or dairy products. We're awfully difficult to cook for!' My friends invariably laugh and say, 'Don't be silly—of course, we want you over! Now, tell me what kinds of things you eat.'

"At that point, I give a few examples of easy-to-make vegan meals, like pasta with marinara sauce or a vegan tostada. I've never had anyone take offense, and they usually thank me for informing them ahead of time.

"Sometimes I offer to bring my own meat substitute, to supplement the side dishes that my friends are cooking for a large dinner party. Last Christmas, for instance, I brought some pre-cooked 'Tofurkey' and ate it right next to my family members who were eating turkey."

Some people are "flexible vegetarians," meaning that they veer away from vegetarianism when their friends serve meat-centered meals. However, most hosts and hostesses appreciate knowing the truth about your diet. In fact, a thoughtful person will ask, "Do you have any food allergies?" before offering to make a meal for a guest.

Becky's Story

"I had been a vegetarian for about 12 years when my neighbor asked, 'Would you like to come over and share our native homeland dish of English Bangers with us?' I had no idea what an English Banger was. I just recall being so taken by her excitement about this dish, and her desire to share it with me that I happily said yes.

"On a beautiful table with English china we were served Brussels sprouts, boiled potatoes, and an English Banger. This is when I discovered that the English Banger is a large, fatty sausage. I quickly pondered the fact that she did not ask me over for Brussels sprouts and boiled potatoes. The only food she mentioned was the English Bangers. So with my hostess grinning from ear to ear, I looked up from my plate, returned the smile, said thank you, and proceeded to eat away on the English Banger.

"I learned a very valuable lesson that night, which is that food has to do with more than just health and wellness. For me, food is also about connecting with people. When asked if I would do it again, I say, 'Yes, in a heartbeat!' In a very rich way, my neighbor was letting me into her life. Prior to this we had only shared pleasantries; and now she was sharing a part of her homeland, a part of who she was, a part of her soul."

There are many variables that affect our choices about what we choose to eat. Tradition, social pressure, tastes, marketing, habits, beliefs—they can all have an influence. The link between vegetarianism and spirituality often involves being flexible in the spirit of kindness. Our inner guidance is a reliable barometer to follow in these situations. Each of us must make our own choices, and know that there is no clear-cut right or wrong decision.

CHAPTER FIVE

Eating Wholesomely

*"We are all God's creatures—that we pray
to God for mercy and justice, while we continue
to eat the flesh of animals that are slaughtered on
our account, is not consistent."*

— ISAAC BASHEVIS SINGER, NOBEL PEACE PRIZE LAUREATE

As a vegetarian or vegan, you've eliminated certain foods from your diet, but it's important to monitor your thoughts and emotions and be aware of any feelings of being "restricted" or "controlled." Even though you're the one who decided to become vegan, you may begin to resent your lifestyle.

Resentment stems from negative thoughts such as: "Oh, darn, I can't eat that food." To release the negativity and frustration, simply focus on the advantages that come from your vegetarian lifestyle. Reframe your thoughts with empowering affirmations such as:

- *Eating fresh fruits and vegetables energizes me for hours.*

- *I feel good about the way my eating patterns help animals and the environment.*

- *I love how my eating habits affect my fitness and figure.*

- *I'm saying yes to health and energy by eating this way.*

Be sure to eat a lot of different types of food, as variety will prevent you from getting bored with veganism. Eating a diverse array of foods will also help you ingest the nutrients you need. You might subscribe to *Vegetarian Times* or take out vegan cookbooks from the library in order to learn new recipes. Also, many community colleges, health-food stores, and restaurants offer vegan cooking classes. And, check to see if Earth-Save International or the Vegan Society meets in your area (see the Resources section of this book). These organizations offer support and information for vegans.

Eating at Restaurants and On-the-Go

One way to ensure that you'll enjoy a variety of delicious vegan meals is by eating out, but many new vegans feel unsure about what to order.

Doreen: With my busy workshop schedule, I travel nearly every weekend. I've learned how to maintain my vegan lifestyle, no matter what type of restaurant I'm in. Here are some tips that I've learned while on the road:

Always inform your waiter or waitress that you are a vegetarian or vegan, and ask for their help in making food selections. Also, be on the lookout for hidden sources of animal products on the menu, such as pastas or soups that are made with a chicken-broth stock. Don't be afraid to ask your food server to check with the chef to see: (1) if animal products are used in the food preparation; and (2) if substitute ingredients can be used. I've never had a waiter or waitress refuse this request, and they always warmly answer my questions and give me help.

For example, if you're at an Italian restaurant, watch for egg-based pasta; sauce made with cream, cheese, and/or butter; and cheese- or meat-filled ravioli. Ask that your pasta be made with marinara sauce, which is a vegan red sauce; or with olive oil, garlic, and basil. Some fast-food pizza restaurants use beef stock in their marinara sauce, so ask your waiter for an ingredients list for the red sauce. If you're a vegan, clearly specify that you don't want cheese in, or on top of, your meal. I've grown to love vegan pizza, which is made with red sauce, vegetables, and no cheese. Another favorite of mine is bruschetta, which consists of sourdough bread, basil, and chopped roma tomatoes.

Asian restaurants offer the largest variety of vegan meals. Chinese, Thai, and Vietnamese establishments serve many delicious vegetable dishes. I love freshly sautéed or steamed vegetables. Be sure to specify that you want a vegan sauce on the vegetables. Some Asian restaurants cover their vegetables with sauce made from oyster, beef, or chicken stock. Also, check that the soup is vegetable-based. Unfortunately, most Asian restaurants serve soup that has fish stock, freeze-dried fish powder, or chicken stock as a base of their miso, hot-and-sour, and egg-drop soups. Other delicious choices include vegan spring rolls, vegetable chow mein, and pad thai noodle dishes.

At Japanese restaurants, you can also enjoy a variety of vegan dishes. Try a cucumber or seaweed salad topped with ginger or miso dressing. One of my favorites is "Avocado Sushi." This is just like a California roll, with nori-maki (the flat, green seaweed used to wrap sushi rolls), rice, and avocado inside. Most sushi bars don't have this on the menu but are happy to make it if you order it. Vegan sushi rolls, made with cucumber, radish, and carrot slices, are available at most Japanese restaurants these days. You can also make a meal of a rice bowl (ask for brown rice, if available) with teriyaki-cooked vegetables on top. Tempura vegetables are delicious but can be high in fat.

At Mexican restaurants, you'll need to inquire whether their beans are made with lard. Many Mexican restaurants offer vegan beans, and this can be the basis for a variety of healthful and low-fat meals. For instance, you can enjoy a vegan bean burrito, tostada salad, taco, or enchilada. If the beans are made with lard, use the restaurant's Spanish rice as a basis for your meal. Just be sure to check that the rice isn't cooked in chicken stock and that the tortillas aren't made with lard. For vegans, you don't want cheese and sour cream as part of your meals. Ask for guacamole as a substitute for cheese and sour cream so that the meal isn't too dry—and it will also "cool off" the hot salsa-based flavor. Gazpacho soup and meat-free nachos are other delicious vegan choices to enjoy at Mexican restaurants. Do avoid corn products unless you can verify that they're non-GMO.

At American or steak-and-seafood restaurants, you'll need to be a little more creative. Most of the "garden salads" offered at these places consist of little more than a sad chunk of iceberg lettuce. Again, rely on the food server's knowledge of the menu to help you order. Remember, too, that you can make very satisfying meals from side dishes—for example, a baked potato with olive oil; steamed or grilled vegetables (hold the butter and cheese); baked beans; rice with vegetables (inquire whether their rice pilaf has a chicken-stock base); or a vegan noodle dish.

Fast-food eateries now cater to health-conscious consumers; and offer salads, baked potatoes, and veggie burgers. Check the ingredients labels on fast-food salad dressings, however, as many of them have "gelatin," made from cow's bones and muscles. Better to squeeze some lemon juice and sprinkle salt and pepper on your salad, rather than eat gelatin-based dressing.

Since fast-food restaurants are usually located in clusters, you can leave one restaurant for another if they don't offer a vegan meal. In a pinch for fast food, opt for a whole-wheat bagel and a piece of fruit (sold at many coffee shops) instead. Grocery stores are another avenue for eating on the run. You can grab a bag of organic carrots and dip them into hummus bean dip, or snack on a banana, an avocado, a watermelon, or some nuts. Most delis, including fast-food chains, can make you a vegan sandwich consisting of bread and vegetables.

If you're traveling by plane, call the airline at least 24 hours prior to your flight to request a vegan meal. Most airlines cater to the different types of vegetarians, so you can specifically request a meal with, for instance, "no dairy," "no beef," or "no fish." I've learned the hard way that when you depend upon a travel agent to request special meals, you often don't receive them. It's better to call the airline yourself. And just in case your special meal doesn't end up making it to the plane, be sure to pack some vegan snacks such as organic rice cakes, fruit, or trail mix. The airlines allow you to carry one extra bag that is completely filled with food for immediate consumption, as long as there are no liquids that you bought outside of the airport. Most flight attendants are creative when it comes to making an impromptu vegan meal out of side dishes and a combination of first-class and coach-class meal items—if you explain your situation to them.

Vitamin and Mineral Supplements

Should vegans supplement their diets by taking vitamins? For most, the answer is yes. Vegans, in particular, need to take B_{12} for three main reasons: The amount of B_{12} in our soil and on our crops has been altered due to our modern way of growing and harvesting food; processed food ends up leaving us with less B_{12}; and finally, a compound called "analogs" may be present in food, instead of B_{12}. These analogs look like B_{12}, but do none of the functions of B_{12}, so when they hook into a B_{12} position in the body, they occupy the space without doing the job. And if you are a vegan who doesn't get out in the sun very much, you'll need to supplement your diet with vitamins D and K, too. (Vitamin K helps you to assimilate vitamin D.)

Nutritional research began with a focus on the prevention of disease. Many of the discoveries of specific vitamins and minerals were found because people had developed a disease state that the vitamin or mineral would repair.

Today, the focus of nutritional studies is on supporting optimal health. Every day, scientists discover new information in this regard. In the future, we will develop a solid foundation about what promotes optimal health, but in the meantime, we're like guinea pigs when we self-supplement in megadose ranges.

The recommended daily allowances (RDAs) focus only on the prevention of nutritional deficiencies in population groups; they do not define optimal intake for an individual. The RDAs also do not adequately take into consideration environmental and lifestyle factors that can destroy vitamins and minerals (smoking, alcohol, food additives, heavy metals, and carbon monoxide). With this said, the following are some practical recommendations to help you design a basic nutritional supplement program:

1. **Take a high-quality multiple vitamin-and-mineral supplement.**

2. **Take extra antioxidants.** This is an important supplement to a diet rich in plant foods, especially fruits and vegetables. Mixtures of antioxidant nutrients appear to work together harmoniously to produce the phenomenon of synergy. The two primary antioxidants in the human body are vitamins C and E. Be sure to recognize how much your multiple vitamin-and-mineral formula provides. The daily supplementation guidelines for these key nutritional antioxidants for supporting general

health is vitamin E (d-alpha tocopherol): 400 to 800
IU; and vitamin C (ascorbic acid): 500 to 1,500 mg.

3. **Take one tablespoon of unrefined flaxseed oil
   daily**, which is considered by many experts to be
   the answer to restoring the proper level of essential fatty acids.

Going too far in either direction is not necessarily nutritionally better. A few of the popular extremes
in recent years include eating no fat at all; consuming two to four times the amount of protein that is
needed; and taking a high-level dose of vitamin and
mineral supplements.

Just as our blood has a pH balance with either
side being too acidic or too basic, our immune system
has a balance, too. When we take too high or too low
of an intake of vitamin and minerals, our immune
system is stressed. And when our immune system is
stressed, we are more prone to illness. Moderation is
an important key.

When choosing vitamins, read the label for hidden animal ingredients. Avoid gelatin capsules, which,
as we previously mentioned, are made from cow bone
and muscle; and vitamins derived from fish, beef,
or dairy by-products. Most health-food stores offer

Eating Wholesomely

vitamins made specifically for vegetarians. They are clearly marked "Suitable for Vegetarians," or simply, "Vegan." Do your best to choose organic vitamins, especially vitamin C, which is made from corn.

You can also supplement your diet with vegan protein powders. Drink smoothies made with fresh fruit, nonfat vanilla oat or almond milk, and a scoop of protein powder. Most of the powders (available at health-food stores) contain a wide variety of vitamin and minerals. Be aware of double-supplementing with a multivitamin or a shake. Another item to add to the shake, in place of the protein powder, is soft tofu, which will make your shake creamy and thick, while also providing a protein source. If you are a vegan, check the ingredients list on protein powders to ensure that they're not made with milk or whey products.

As far as supplements, the American Dietetic Association says:

Both vegetarian and vegan diets can provide completely adequate nutrition that foster good health. There is nothing inherently wrong with either one. If you choose to eliminate only meat from your diet, you must find suitable plant replacements for some nutrients.

If you choose to eliminate dairy products as well, you need to consider a few more nutrients. When you eliminate all foods of animal origin . . . vegans must rely on fortified foods or nutritional supplements.

Daily Nutritional Suggestions for Vegans

Many of us learned about the "food groups" in grade school. Based on the nutritional beliefs of that time, our teachers said that we needed to eat meat and dairy products to be healthy.

Today we know better! We now have a tool called the "Food Pyramid" to help guide our daily decisions about what to eat for optimal health. Here are suggestions for your daily meal selections, modified for vegans. Next to each food category, we've listed how many servings the Food Pyramid recommends that you eat daily. Below each food category, we've listed examples of what would constitute a single serving:

— **Fats, oils, and sweets:** use sparingly

🖉 ⅛ of an avocado

🖉 1 tsp oil

- 1 tsp butter or margarine

- 2 Tbsp of half-and-half

- 1 Tbsp salad dressing

- 2 Tbsp reduced-fat salad dressing

— Dry beans, nuts, seeds, eggs, and meat substitutions: 2–3 servings daily

- Organic soy milk: 1 cup

- Cooked dry beans or peas: ½ cup

- Nuts or seeds: 2 Tbsp

- Organic tofu or tempeh: ¼ cup

- Peanut or almond butter: 2 Tbsp

— Vegetables: 3–5 servings daily

- Cooked or chopped raw vegetables: ½ cup

- Raw leafy vegetables: 1 cup

— Fruits: 2–4 servings daily

- Juice: ½ cup

- Dried fruit: ¼ cup

- Chopped raw fruit: ½ cup

🖉 1 medium-size piece of fruit, such as a
banana, apple, or orange

— **Breads:** 6–11 servings daily

🖉 Bagel: ½

🖉 Bread: 1 slice

🖉 Cooked cereal: ½ cup

🖉 Cooked organic rice, pasta, or other grains:
½ cup

Nutritional Considerations

As mentioned earlier, there are three types of nutrients in food: fats, carbohydrates, and protein. Many
popular diets and cultural myths have created confusion about these nutritional properties. When going vegan, it's even more important to get the facts
straight.

Fats

Some people are attracted to the idea of a no-fat
diet, although it really is true that "fat is our friend."
However, for some of us, we have made fat too much
of a bosom buddy! Eating less fat is a great idea, but
having no fat in the diet is silly and dangerous. The

functions of fat in the body are numerous:

- 🖋 Fat is used by the body for energy.

- 🖋 Fat provides insulation that keeps us warm.

- 🖋 Fats carry and store fat-soluble vitamins.

- 🖋 The essential fatty acids, linolenic and linoleic, are only obtained by the fat we eat.

- 🖋 All of the cells of our body are composed of a fat/protein layer.

- 🖋 Eating fat helps us to feel full and satisfied.

When we don't eat enough fat, we come up short in all those areas. Ten percent fat in the diet is a worthy goal, but most people have a hard time sticking to this level. Twenty percent fat is healthy and more manageable. However, the average person currently gets about 40 percent of their calories from fat.

As a vegan, you may begin eating excessive amounts of dairy products. If they are the full-fat, or even the low-fat, variety, your fat-gram percentage can easily add up. Also watch out for the trap of thinking that "no-fat" items are noncaloric. Excess calories from anything—including healthful and vegan foods—put weight on us if the calories exceed our daily needs.

Carbohydrates

Eating healthfully also means avoiding or reducing the amount of sugar in your diet. Sugars are in the family of carbohydrates. There are simple and complex carbohydrates. Table sugar, honey, and molasses are examples of simple carbohydrates. Bread, rice, beans, and potatoes are examples of complex carbohydrates.

Fruits and vegetables fall in between. When we turn fruits and vegetables into juice, they act more like simple carbohydrates. When we leave them in their natural state, they lean in the direction of being complex carbohydrates. Eating fewer simple carbohydrates, such as sugar, honey, or molasses, is a very good idea.

Before we go any further, let's dispel the myth that breads make you fat. Carbohydrates are not fattening in and of themselves. What we put on them makes them fattening. Bread has a minimal amount of fat, but if you add butter, you add fat. Pasta is not fattening, but put Alfredo sauce on top and you have a fatty dish. Replace the Alfredo sauce with a marinara sauce and you're back to a low-fat dish. A baked potato has no fat, but when you add butter, sour cream, or cheese, the fat grams add up.

Some carbohydrates drawn from processed foods are high in fat—such as chips, fries, croissants, muffins, and doughnuts. Just remember that carbohydrates, like fats, are our friends. They provide us with the energy to live, to think, and to move. Focus on eating the complex carbohydrates from breads, cereal, pasta, rice, potatoes, and beans. Limit eating those that are simple carbohydrates, such as cookies, cakes, pies, and ice cream.

Proteins

The average person eats two to four times the amount of animal sources of protein that they need. The amount of protein recommended for healthy adults is 0.36 grams protein per pound of body weight. The recommended intake for an adult woman or man weighing 135 pounds is 0.36 x 135 = 49 grams protein (or a little less than 2 ounces of protein). This includes a safety margin, and can be expected to be above the actual needs of almost all 135-pound individuals. The recommended intake for an adult weighing 189 pounds is 0.36 x 180 = 65 grams protein (or about 2½ ounces of protein).

To give you a visual sense of this, three ounces is the size of a deck of cards. See the section, "Meeting

Protein Requirements" on page 112 for other examples of how to meet your protein needs.

If you're a vegan, eating at least one to two cups of cooked beans daily will help to ensure that you receive enough protein (one of these two cups can come from making a smoothie with one cup of soft organic tofu blended in).

If you eat eggs, milk, cheese, yogurt, fish, turkey, or chicken, you don't need to worry about adequate protein. The more you restrict or eliminate animal sources of food in your diet, the greater the need to complement your proteins.

Some Final Points on Proteins

— **Classifying proteins as incomplete or complete is misleading.** All plant proteins are complete. They provide all the essential amino acids needed for health, just in varying amounts. We generally think of meat and other animal foods as the best sources of protein, but in fact, a plant-based diet can easily meet our protein needs.

— **"Protein combining" means eating a variety of protein-rich foods throughout the day** (for example, several servings daily of grains, beans, vegetables, and nuts or seeds). The proteins in these foods combine with the body's own natural-forming pool of amino acids (known as "endogenous amino acids") in the body to provide adequate, high-quality protein.

— **Eating combinations of plant foods helps improve the overall quality of the proteins in those foods.**

— **Consuming adequate calories is important for meeting protein needs.** When caloric intake is inadequate, protein needs increase.

— **Almost without exception, everyone, including vegans, consumes more protein than they require.** There is no advantage to eating excess protein.

Meeting Protein Requirements
(based on 1,800 calories/day)

Food Group	Serving Size	Protein (gm/serving)	Servings (per day)	Protein (total gm)
Bread/starchy vegetables*	½ cup or 1 slice	3	10	30
Bean, peas, and lentils	½ cup	7	3	21
Vegetables (non-starchy)	½ cup	2	5	10
Fruit	½ cup or 1 medium cup	.5	4	2
Milk	8 fl oz	8	2	16
Fats/oils	Varies	0	4	0

* Examples of starchy vegetables include potatoes, yams, sweet potatoes, corn, baked beans, mixed vegetables (corn and peas), plantains, and squash (acorn or butternut).

Protein Equivalents of Plant Foods

Here is a list of vegan foods that provide 10 to 16 grams of protein:

 Bread: 4 slices (12 grams)

 Brown rice: 2 cups cooked (10 grams)

⬧ Green whole organic soybeans: 1 cup cooked (14 grams)

⬧ Pasta: 2 cups cooked (12 grams)

⬧ Sesame seeds: ¼ cup (10 grams)

⬧ Organic soy milk: 1½ cups (10 grams)

⬧ Sunflower seeds: ½ cup (16 grams)

⬧ Organic tofu: ½ cup (10 grams)

Vitamin D

Throughout history, being exposed to the sun has provided us with adequate amounts of vitamin D. People with lighter skin color require about 20 to 30 minutes of sun exposure a day (avoiding peak hours, of course), to make adequate amounts of vitamin D. People with greater pigmentation and darker skin color require greater exposure time to make a similar amount of vitamin D.

However, smog, sunscreen, living in northern latitudes, or spending less time outdoors all lead to less sun exposure. For these reasons, fortified foods are usually necessary to provide dietary vitamin D.

A regular source of dietary vitamin D is recommended for those who don't get enough sun exposure, or who have darker skin. Milk is fortified with vitamin D, as are as some brands of soy milk, rice milk, and many commercial cereals. Be sure to take a vitamin K supplement, which helps us to assimilate vitamin D.

Vitamin B_6

Vitamin B_6 needs are closely linked to protein intake, since it functions with more than 60 enzymes to help with amino-acid metabolism. Because vegans consume less total animal protein than omnivores, they don't need to metabolize amino acids as much. Therefore, they need less vitamin B_6. The ratio of vitamin B_6 to protein in plant foods is actually superior to that of animal foods. Vitamin B_6, found in plants, is also more stable than the forms found in animal-based foods.

Some people are concerned about the controversy surrounding a high-fiber diet, and the metabolism of vitamin B_6. However, studies show that, in most populations, a high fiber intake doesn't seem to interfere with B_6 status. Vitamin B_6 is found among different groups of plant foods. Good sources include many ready-to-eat cereals, potatoes, bananas, figs, chickpeas, soybeans, and brewer's yeast.

Minerals

Most minerals are widely available in a plant-based vegan diet; however, three minerals are an exception: calcium, iron, and zinc. You'll need to be aware which foods have these minerals to ensure that you ingest adequate nutrients.

Calcium

Vegan foods that provide calcium include the following:

- Calcium-fortified foods (organic soy or rice milk, orange juice, etc.)
- Calcium-sulfate processed organic tofu (look on the label for it)
- Blackstrap molasses
- Organic soy yogurt
- Sesame seeds and almonds
- Dark leafy greens (collards, kale, mustard greens)
- Nuts and seeds
- Lime-processed organic tortillas
- Legumes

Most lacto-ovo vegetarians usually meet or exceed their calcium needs. Studies show that when you eat animal protein, you need to consume more calcium. Therefore, vegans need less calcium since they do not eat animal sources of protein. Vegans who consume low-salt diets usually require even less calcium.

Many people worry that if they don't have enough calcium, they'll suffer from osteoporosis. Yet healthy bones are ensured by many factors other than diet:

- Regular physical activity, especially weight-bearing exercise, such as running, bicycling, or working out with weights

- Adequate sun exposure or consuming vitamin D–fortified foods

- Avoiding excess consumption of sodium

- Eating plant foods on a daily basis that are rich in calcium and vitamin D–fortified foods

- Genetic factors (whether your family members have had bone-related issues)

- Factors such as avoiding high intakes of salt, alcohol, caffeine, and animal protein; and avoiding a sedentary lifestyle

Two Ways to Ensure Having Strong Bones

1. Consume calcium-rich foods and beverages, including the following:

- Dark green vegetables, such as broccoli, collards, bok choy, Chinese cabbage, or kale

- Calcium-fortified organic tofu

- Nuts and sesame seeds

- Asian foods, such as sushi, made with the seaweed nori or nori-maki, or other sea vegetables such as hijiki or dried seaweed

- Foods labeled "calcium-fortified," such as orange juice

2. Exercise regularly, combining cardiovascular conditioning exercises and weight-bearing exercises such as power-walking, jogging, cycling, stair-climbing, or working with stationary weight equipment at a gym.

Food Choices That
Meet the RDA for Calcium

Food	Calcium Content (mg)
½ cup cooked brown rice	10
1 slice whole-wheat bread	20
English muffin	92
½ cup cooked broccoli	89
½ cup cooked collards	178
½ cup tofu	120 to 350
1 cup cooked beans	86
2 Tbsp almond butter	86
3 cups soy milk	252
1 Tbsp blackstrap molasses	187
1 orange	56
Total	1,176 to 1,406

Iron

Nutritional sources of iron include the following:

- Iron-fortified breakfast cereals

- Organic tofu

- Whole grains

- Legumes

🍃 Green, leafy vegetables

🍃 Dried fruits

Foods contain two forms of iron: *heme* and *non-heme*. Heme iron is only in animal products such as beef; while non-heme iron is in plant foods such as whole grains, legumes, nuts, and seeds. Recent research shows some advantages to consuming iron mostly, or totally, in the form of non-heme iron.

The recommended daily allowance (RDA) for iron for adult men and women is 10 mg, and 15 mg, respectively.

Vitamin C can enhance non-heme iron absorption. Seventy-five mg of vitamin C, found in five ounces of orange juice, can enhance iron absorption from a meal by as much as a factor of four. To have this benefit, the vitamin C source and iron must be consumed at about the same time.

Phytates (whole grains and legumes), oxalates, and/or tannins (in tea and Indian spices: turmeric, coriander, chilies, and tamarind) all decrease the absorption of non-heme iron. The good news is an intake of 25 to 75 mg of vitamin C (found in ¼ to ½ cup orange juice) increases the absorption of non-heme iron two- to four-fold. Legumes also inhibit iron absorption, but this, too, can be minimized by the intake of vitamin C.

Two Steps to Help Ensure Adequate Iron Intake and Iron Stores of the Body

1. Eat foods that are rich in iron, such as fortified cereals, organic tofu, whole grains, and legumes.

2. Eat foods that are rich in vitamin C, such as citrus fruits, berries, broccoli, cauliflower, and dark-green leafy vegetables.

Zinc

Most (70 percent) of the zinc in the American diet comes from animal products, meat in particular. Despite this, Western vegans tend to receive enough zinc. Plant sources of zinc include whole grains, nuts, organic tofu, and legumes.

The Bottom Line

The bottom line is to increase your intake of whole-grain products, low-fat dairy products, and fruits and vegetables; while decreasing your intake of fried and fatty meats, high-salt foods, high-sugar foods, and high-protein foods.

You Can Do It

Sometimes people feel intimidated about shopping at health-food and specialty stores, so they stick with their traditional grocery store out of habit, and because it feels "safe." They worry about feeling comfortable in a new type of store, and wonder whether they'll be confused by exotic product names.

We have found that health-food stores (also known as bio stores and whole-food stores in various areas of the world) have a warm and loving ambiance that is lacking in traditional supermarkets. Health-food stores feel calmer, while supermarkets can feel chaotic. Since food absorbs the energy of its surroundings, we rarely choose to shop at a supermarket.

The greatest advantage of health-food store shopping is the large selection of organic produce. Yes, organics cost a little more than supermarket produce, but how often have you bought fruits or vegetables and found them wilted in your refrigerator in no time? Or perhaps you didn't eat the produce because it was tasteless, as most supermarket produce is picked before it's ripe.

Health-food store produce, in contrast, is rich in flavor and nutrients. Not only is it vine-ripened, but organic farming creates rich soil. The soil, in turn, stimulates the plant to produce fruits and vegetables that are loaded with vitamins, minerals, fiber, and flavor. So, the extra cost is an investment in buying produce that you'll be motivated to eat.

"But I can't use coupons on the brands of foods sold at health-food stores!" the budget-conscious consumer might protest. Yes, but how are those commercial brands of foods affecting your family's mental and physical health? Look at the ingredients on the foods that you can get for 50 cents off, with a coupon. Most likely, the foods are filled with preservatives, sugar, and artificial coloring. Think of how those additives affect your children's behavior, and you'll see that the more expensive natural foods will save you time, money, and headaches in the long run.

In addition, if you or your family still eat meat or dairy products, you'll find a wide variety of organic and free-range animal products at health-food stores. The meat, eggs, cheeses, milk, sour cream, and ice cream come from animals who are humanely treated. They are also free of growth hormones, GMOs, pesticides, and other unwanted additives.

Most health-food stores employ knowledgeable personnel who can help you select vitamin and mineral supplements. They also offer "cruelty-free" beauty and bath items. Many commercial soaps and makeups have animal ingredients, or they were tested on animals in inhumane ways. Your vegan lifestyle incorporates more than what you eat. It also includes choosing toiletries and cleaning supplies that are free of animal products and that are environmentally sound.

You can find the nearest health-food store by do-ing an Internet search with the keywords "health foods," "bio shop," "organic," or "whole foods." You may want to call ahead to inquire which particular store offers produce, a deli, or the ingredients you're looking for. When shopping at a new store, it's helpful to bring a grocery list. You can create your list from a recipe, or just by looking in your cupboards and seeing what's needed.

Go shopping when the store first opens in the morning, or a few hours before closing time. Those tend to be non-peak customer times, which will save you time. The store personnel will also be freer to assist you when they're not so busy.

If your town doesn't have a health-food store, you can ask the manager of your local grocery store to order items for you. Many grocery stores now have a section for organic produce and health-food items. Another option is to buy products from the online stores on health-food websites or home-delivery co-ops. (listed in the Resources section of this book).

Cooking and Substitutions

Variety in your meals creates balance, which is a key to vitality. This means eating some foods raw and others cooked, while minimizing your intake of fatty, sugary, and salty foods.

Here are some substitutions you can use while cooking to make your ingredients from vegan products:

Animal Product Ingredient	Vegetarian Substitutions
1 cup milk	1 cup soy or rice milk
1 egg	2-inch square of tofu (blended), or 1 Tbsp soy flour and 1 Tbsp water, or ¼ cup egg substitute, or ½ mashed banana, or ⅓ cup applesauce or canned pumpkin, or 2 Tbsp cornstarch
1 cup ricotta cheese	1 cup firm tofu (mashed)
1 cup yogurt	1 cup tofu (blended)
1 Tbsp butter	1 Tbsp applesauce or fruit puree, or 1 Tbsp soy margarine

Eggs are called for in recipes because they "bind" the ingredients together as they cook. Some vegan binders that you can use instead of eggs include applesauce, mashed potatoes, fine bread crumbs, or cooked oatmeal. You can also substitute the dairy products called for in recipes. Health-food stores sell organic soy-, rice-, and almond-based versions of sour cream, mayonnaise, salad dressing, and yogurt. Some cheese substitutes have casein in their ingredients. Since casein is a milk by-product, vegans will want to steer clear of it and read the ingredients list.

You can make your kitchen "vegan-friendly" by having staple ingredients on hand. For instance, keep vegetable broth or vegetable bouillon cubes handy to make a rice pilaf or soup dish. To add a little spice in a hurry, make sure that your cupboard is always stocked with balsamic vinegar, peanut sauce, barbecue sauce, soy sauce/tamari, mustard, ketchup, and hot sauce. Keep meat substitutes in stock to help out in a pinch, such as frozen veggie burgers, organic tofu dogs, organic soy sausage, and veggie deli slices. Develop the habit of automatically buying organic broccoli, lettuce, carrots, and other vegetables. Many health-food stores sell pre-chopped or shredded vegetables, which are real time-savers at home.

Suggestions for Fast Vegan Meals and Snacks

  ✐ A bagel with almond butter and a piece of fruit

- Canned vegetable soup, with salad and bread

- Rice pilaf, using an organic packaged mix from a health-food store, tossed with steamed mixed vegetables

- A bran muffin and fruit juice

- Trail mix and fruit juice

- Spaghetti with prepared organic sauce

- Bean burritos using canned beans and chopped heirloom tomatoes

Guidelines for Reducing Fat in Vegan Meals

Reduce your use of fatty spreads, such as butter, margarine, and peanut butter, by using the following:

- Bean spreads made from cooked beans pureed with chopped onions and celery, herbs, and lemon juice or salsa

- Fruit spreads made by pureeing dried fruits with a small amount of water or fruit juice

- Low-fat organic tofu blended with herbs and lemon juice to make a dip or sandwich spread

🖉 You can reduce the fat in homemade baked goods by cutting the oil or margarine in a recipe by 25 percent or more. Or, replace some of the fat in a baked product with mashed bananas, blended tofu, or pureed prunes. Because fat intensifies flavors, it may be necessary to increase the amounts of vanilla extract or spices in low-fat baked goods.

Here are some other ways to reduce the fat in your vegan meals:

🖉 Sauté onions and other vegetables in recipes in vegetable broth, tomato juice, or apple juice instead of oil.

🖉 Flavor dishes with nonfat flavor enhancer, such as sun-dried tomatoes, fresh ginger, freshly squeezed lemon or lime juice, and fresh herbs.

🖉 Use low-fat organic tofu in place of regular tofu in recipes.

🖉 Blend low-fat organic tofu to add to dishes that call for cream; or thicken soups or sauces with blended vegetables, legumes, or mashed potatoes.

🖉 🖉 🖉

Optimal Intake Range for Vitamins and Minerals

"Whenever we cause suffering or death to any other being, we cause suffering to the Great Life Force."

— SHIK PO CHIH

Vitamin Range for Adults

Vitamin A* (from beta-carotene): 5,000–25,000 IU
Vitamin A (retinol): 5,000 IU
Vitamin B$_1$ (thiamin): 10–100 mg

Vitamin B$_2$ (riboflavin): 10–50 mg

Vitamin B$_6$ (pyridoxine): 25–100 mg

Vitamin B$_{12}$ (cobalamin): 400 mcg

Biotin: 100–300 mg

Vitamin C (ascorbic acid): 100–1,000 mg

Choline: 10–100 mg

Vitamin D: 100–400 IU

Vitamin E** (d-alpha tocopherol): 100–800 mg

Folic Acid: 400 mcg

Inositol: 10–100 mg

Vitamin K (phytonadione): 60–300 mcg

Niacin: 10–100 mg

Niacinamide: 10–30 mg

Pantothenic Acid: 25–100 mg

*Women of childbearing age should not take more than 2,500 IU of vitamin A daily if becoming pregnant is a possibility, due to the risk of birth defects.

**Elderly people in nursing homes who live in northern latitudes should supplement vitamin E at the high end of the range.

Mineral Range for Adults

Boron: 1–6 mg

Calcium: 250–1,500 mg

Chromium: 200–400 mcg

Copper: 1–2 mg

Iodine: 50–150 mcg
Iron: 15–30 mg
Magnesium: 250–500 mg
Manganese: 10–15 mg
Molybdenum: 10–25 mcg
Potassium: 200–500 mg
Selenium: 100–200 mcg
Silica 1: 25 mg
Vanadium: 50–100 mcg
Zinc: 15–45 mg

(From *Encyclopedia of Natural Medicine,* by M. Murray and J. Pizzorno, Prima Publishing, 1998.)

🖋 🖋 🖋

Care of the Earth

"If we eat the flesh of living creatures,
we are destroying the seeds of compassion."

— FROM THE SURANGAMA SUTRA, A BUDDHIST TEXT

Eating animals has an enormously detrimental impact on our environment. What follows are a few recent findings provided through EarthSave International:

— The United Nations reports that because of over-fishing, all 17 of the world's major fishing areas have reached or exceeded their natural limits.

— Like fisheries, rangelands almost everywhere are being grazed at or beyond their sustainable yields.

Livestock grazing harms roughly 20 percent of all threatened and endangered species in the United States.

— Beef production in Latin America, for both domestic and international markets, fuels the destruction of irreplaceable rain forests. On October 12, 1995, the *New York Times* reported, "Burning in the Amazon appears to be approaching the worst levels ever." Clearing forests to create cattle pasture is a principal cause of fires.

— Fertilizers, pesticides, and other runoff from Midwestern farms (most of which grow grain for farm animals) have created a massive, lifeless expanse in the Gulf of Mexico. In 1995, this so-called dead zone reached 40,000 square miles, roughly the size of New Jersey. Recall that 70 percent of U.S. grain is fed to livestock, and the connections between our food choices and such environmental tragedies become readily apparent.

— Thirty-eight percent of world grain production, 70 percent of United States grain, and one-third of the world's fish catch are fed directly to livestock. In Mexico, where 22 percent of citizens suffer from malnutrition, 30 percent of all grain is fed to livestock.

— Producing one pound of feedlot beef takes up to 2,500 gallons of water and about 12 pounds of grain. It takes six pounds of grain and up to 660 gallons of water to produce one pound of chicken. To produce one egg requires three gallons of water.

— Eighty-five percent of U.S. topsoil is lost from cropland, pasture, rangeland, and forestland due to raising livestock.

— Almost half the energy used in American agriculture goes into producing livestock.

— The manure produced by farm animals in the U.S. is roughly ten times the waste produced by all the country's human residents. Belgium, the Netherlands, and France now produce more animal manure than their land can absorb.

— Every year in South and Central America, five million acres of rain forest are felled to create cattle pasture.

— The European appetite for imported frog legs has decimated frog populations in India and Bangladesh.

— The price of meat would double or triple if the full ecological costs—including fossil fuel use, groundwater depletion, and agricultural-chemical pollution were included in the price tag.

— Pounds of edible product that can be produced on an acre of land:

- Cherries: 5,000

- Green beans: 10,000

- Apples: 20,000

- Carrots: 30,000

- Potatoes: 40,000

- Tomatoes: 50,000

- Celery: 60,000

- Beef: 250

Your pocketbook, and what you choose to buy, greatly impacts the environment. There's a theory called "the hundredth monkey concept," which says that when a certain number of us adopt a healthful habit, the whole world becomes "weighted" in that healthful direction. In other words, everyone benefits by that percentage of the population who acts healthfully. Using that hundredth monkey concept, as soon as enough people decide to reduce, drastically decrease, or eliminate animal sources of food in their diet, we will see a tremendous healing of the earth. The earth, just like your body, is very forgiving, and it wants to heal.

Resources

Compassion Couture: An online store selling vegan shoes, boots, bags, belts, and other accessories that are normally leather. Compassion Couture strives to only sell eco-friendly and fair-trade goods.
Website: www.compassioncoutureshop.com

Cri de Coeur: An online store selling fair-trade vegan designer shoes, boots, and bags.
Website: www.cri-de-coeur.com

EarthSave International: EarthSave International leads a global movement of people from all walks of life who are taking concrete steps to promote healthy and life-sustaining food choices. EarthSave supplies information, support, and practical programs to those who have learned that their food choices impact environmental and human health. Many local chapters have active social and singles clubs.
Website: www.earthsave.org

Fooducate: A resource website and app that helps you avoid genetically modified organisms (GMOs) in your food, beverages, and environment.
Website: www.fooducate.com

Green Polka Dot Box: Organic non-GMO food and goods are delivered to your home (U.S. only).

Website: www.greenpolkadotbox.com

Happy Cow: A website and app that lists vegan *and* vegetarian restaurants and stores worldwide, including consumer reviews.

Website: www.happycow.net

Leaping Bunny: A consumer website that lists makeup and personal-care products that have not been tested on animals and which contain no animal ingredients.

Website: www.leapingbunny.org

MooShoes: The manufacturer and Internet store for women's and men's Novacas (which means "no cow" in Spanish) brand boots and shoes, which are vegan, fashionable, comfortable, eco-friendly, and fair-trade. MooShoes also sells vegan purses, belts, wallets, and tablet covers. Be sure to visit their store if in you're in New York City, and meet their shop kitty cat!

Website: www.mooshoes.com

New Zealand Vegetarian Society: A New Zea-land–based organization featuring vegetarian or

vegan nutritional information, food ideas, and vegetarian events.

Website: www.vegetarian.org.nz

NoMeat.com: An Internet resource for information about vegetarianism, and for purchasing meat
substitutes.

Website: www.nomeat.com

North American Vegetarian Society: An organization of regional vegetarian societies. This group has the
names and contact information for the vegetarian club
close to you. Joining a vegetarian club can help you
during your transition to vegetarianism because you
will receive support from other members, as well as
practical tips and information. Log on to their website
and hit the "Affiliates" link to find the vegetarian society nearest to you.

Website: www.navs-online.org • *Phone:* (518) 568-
7970

Novacas: A European shoe and boot manufacturer offering stylish footwear that is vegan, eco-friendly,
and fair-trade. The word *novacas* is Spanish for "no
cows." You can also find their shoes on eBay and
Amazon.

Website: www.novacas.com

100 Percent Pure: Online shopping for vegan and chemical-free shampoo, lotion, makeup, and skin care.
Website: www.100percentpure.com

OlsenHaus: An online store featuring upscale vegan boots, bags, wallets, and shoes.
Website: www.olsenhaus.com

Organics: A great independent site, with product reviews and an explanation of the ABC's of organic farming and eating.
Website: www.organics.org

People for the Ethical Treatment of Animals (PETA): Vegetarian information, from the standpoint of being kind to animals. Contains updates on companies involved in animal testing and experimentation, and gives empowering advice about how we can all help uphold animal rights. PETA is very controversial, but they do help a lot of animals.
Website: www.peta.org

Vegan Action: A website filled with information about becoming a vegan, living a vegan lifestyle, and product reviews.
Website: www.vegan.org

Vegan Backpacker: A wonderful online resource for backpackers worldwide, discussing places to eat vegan food while traveling.

Website: www.veganbackpacker.com

Vegan Society (U.K.): A very helpful British-based organization for vegans. The Internet site provides information on veganism, as well as products.

Website: www.vegansociety.com

Veganz Markets: An all-vegan grocery store and deli in Europe, and hopefully soon in other parts of the world.

Website: www.veganz.de

Vegetarian Resource Group: An Internet resource with practical tips for being a vegetarian, including ideas and an app for those who travel, and lists of vegetarian substitutes for dairy products.

Website: www.vrg.org

VeggieDate: An online dating service for vegetarians and vegans, primarily in North America. Also includes listings of vegetarian events.

Website: www.veggiedate.com

Veggie Hotels: A worldwide online resource of bed-and-breakfast hotels that are vegan-friendly and serve vegan meals.

Website: www.veggie-hotels.com

VegSource: An Internet resource for vegetarian-ism, especially for those who are raising children; with active message boards, links, and information.

Website: www.vegsource.com

Whole Foods Market: A resource to help you find the nearest Whole Foods Market, a leading retailer of organic and healthful food products in the U.S., Canada, and the U.K.

Website: www.wholefoods.com

🌿 🌿 🌿

Bibliography

Berkoff, Nancy, *Vegan in Volume,* The Vegetarian Resource Group, 2000.

Borgstrom, George, Annual meeting of the American Assoc. for the Advancement of Science.

Brown, Judith, *Nutrition Now,* West Publishing, 1995.

Campbell, T. C., *The China Study,* BenBella Books, 2006.

Courtney, Dr. D., Testimony before Senate Commerce Committee Subcommittee on the Environment, Aug. 9, 1974.

EarthSave International's Educational Series #2, © April 1997.

Gustafson, Nancy, *Vegetarian Nutrition,* Nutrition Dimension, 1994.

Havala, S., and Dwyer, J., "Position of the American Dietetic Association: Vegetarian diets." *Journal of the American Dietetic Association,* 1993; Vol. 93: 1317–1319.

Messina, Mark, and Messina, Virginia, *The Dietitian's Guide to Vegetarian Diets,* Aspen Publication, 1996.

Norris, J., *Disease Rates of Vegetarians and Vegans* on Vegan Health.com, 2013.

Physicians Committee for Responsible Medicine, *Vegetarian Starter Kit,* 2013.

Proctor, R., and Thomsen, L., *Veganissimo A–Z*, New York: The Experiment Publishing, 2012.

USDA Economic Research Service, *January–February* 2001 Outlook.

Vegan in Volume, The Complete Vegetarian Cuisine, American Dietetic Association.

"Vegetarian Teens," *Vegetarian Nutrition: A Dietetic Practice Group of the American Dietetic Association,* 1996.

𝒟 𝒟 𝒟

About the Authors

Doreen Virtue holds three university degrees in counseling psychology. A former director of inpatient and outpatient eating disorder units, Doreen has written a number of books and articles on the topic of food cravings, eating disorders, and exercise. She is the author of the best-selling books *The Yo-Yo Diet Syndrome, Constant Craving, The Art of Raw Living Food,* and *Losing Your Pounds of Pain.*

Doreen blends her spiritual background with her psychotherapy training in her workshops and books. She first became a vegetarian at age 17, and has been a complete vegan since 1996. She helps others incorporate veganism into their lives, and lectures on the spiritual benefits of plant-based diets. Doreen is also an avid animal lover and animal-rights advocate.

Doreen has appeared on *Oprah,* CNN, *The View, Good Morning America,* and other programs. Her work has been published in *Redbook, McCall's, Woman's Day, Vegetarian Times, Shape,* and *Fit* magazines, among others.

Website: www.AngelTherapy.com

ANGEL THERAPY®

As a registered dietitian and psychotherapist, **Becky Black** combines her knowledge of food and therapy, focusing on a whole-foods, plant-based approach to nutrition and its impact on wellness and disease prevention. She works with individuals and groups who are seeking to improve their personal health. Becky's other passion is creating contemporary encaustic paintings that have an enriching depth and luminosity.

Website: www.BeckyBlackWaxArt.com

Hay House Titles of Related Interest

YOU CAN HEAL YOUR LIFE, the movie,
starring Louise L. Hay & Friends
(available as a 1-DVD program and an expanded 2-DVD set)
Watch the trailer at: www.LouiseHayMovie.com

THE SHIFT, the movie, starring Dr. Wayne W. Dyer
(available as a 1-DVD program and an expanded 2-DVD set)
Watch the trailer at: www.DyerMovie.com

☞

*CRAZY SEXY KITCHEN: 150 Plant-Empowered Recipes to
Ignite a Mouthwatering Revolution*,
by Kris Carr with Chef Chad Sarno

MINDFUL EATING, by Miraval

THE MYSTIC COOKBOOK: The Secret Alchemy of Food,
by Denise Linn and Meadow Linn

*RAW BASICS: Incorporating Raw Living Foods into Your Diet
Using Easy and Delicious Recipes*, by Jenny Ross

*VEGETARIAN MEALS FOR PEOPLE-ON-THE-GO:
101 Quick & Easy Recipes*, by Vimala Rodgers

All of the above are available at your local bookstore,
or may be ordered by contacting Hay House (see next page).

We hope you enjoyed this Hay House book. If you'd like to receive our online catalog featuring additional information on Hay House books and products, or if you'd like to find out more about the Hay Foundation, please contact:

Hay House, Inc., P.O. Box 5100, Carlsbad, CA 92018-5100
(760) 431-7695 or (800) 654-5126
(760) 431-6948 (fax) or (800) 650-5115 (fax)
www.hayhouse.com® • www.hayfoundation.org

Published and distributed in Australia by: Hay House Australia Pty. Ltd.,
18/36 Ralph St., Alexandria NSW 2015 • *Phone:* 612-9669-4299
Fax: 612-9669-4144 • www.hayhouse.com.au

Published and distributed in the United Kingdom by: Hay House UK, Ltd.,
Astley House, 33 Notting Hill Gate, London W11 3JQ
Phone: 44-20-3675-2450 • *Fax:* 44-20-3675-2451• www.hayhouse.co.uk

Published and distributed in the Republic of South Africa by: Hay House
SA (Pty), Ltd., P.O. Box 990, Witkoppen 2068
Phone/Fax: 27-11-467-8904 • www.hayhouse.co.za

Published in India by: Hay House Publishers India, Muskaan
Complex, Plot No. 3, B-2, Vasant Kunj, New Delhi 110 070
Phone: 91-11-4176-1620 • *Fax:* 91-11-4176-1630 • www.hayhouse.co.in

Distributed in Canada by: Raincoast, 9050 Shaughnessy St., Vancouver,
B.C. V6P 6E5 • *Phone:* (604) 323-7100 • *Fax:* (604) 323-2600
www.raincoast.com

Take Your Soul on a Vacation

Visit www.HealYourLife.com® to regroup, recharge,
and reconnect with your own magnificence.
Featuring blogs, mind-body-spirit news, and
life-changing wisdom from Louise Hay and friends.

Visit www.HealYourLife.com today!